Being ME

A kid's guide to boosting confidence and self-esteem

by Wendy L. Moss, PhD

Magination Press
American Psychological Association
Washington, DC

This book is dedicated to Scott (confident despite adversity). It is also dedicated to all of the children who have given me the opportunity to follow along as they took steps to build confidence and to the children who are now starting out on this journey.—WLM

Published by
MAGINATION PRESS
An Educational Publishing Foundation Book
American Psychological Association
750 First Street, NE
Washington, DC 20002

For more information about our books, including a complete catalog, please write to us, call 1-800-374-2721, or visit our website at www.apa.org/pubs/magination.

Book and cover design by Naylor Design, Inc., Washington, DC
Printed by Worzalla, Stevens Point, Wisconsin

Library of Congress Cataloging-in-Publication Data
Moss, Wendy, Ph. D.
  Being me : a kid's guide to boosting confidence and self-esteem / by Wendy L. Moss.
     p. cm.
  ISBN-13: 978-1-4338-0883-8 (hbk. : alk. paper)
  ISBN-10: 1-4338-0883-8 (hbk. : alk. paper)
  ISBN-13: 978-1-4338-0884-5 (pbk. : alk. paper)
  ISBN-10: 1-4338-0884-6 (pbk. : alk. paper)
  1. Self-confidence—Juvenile literature. 2. Self-esteem—Juvenile literature.
3. Self-confidence in children—Juvenile literature. 4. Self-esteem in children—Juvenile literature. I. Title.
  BF575.S39M67 2011
  155.4'18—dc22
                                                                                    2010014384

First printing September 2010

10 9 8 7 6 5 4 3

Contents

Dear Reader

Do you like being you? Do you have confidence in yourself? Do you believe that there are kids who can like you for who you are and want to hang out with you? If the answer to any of these questions is no, it's important for you to realize that you are not alone. There are a lot of kids, probably many who you are in school with, who wish that they felt more confident. When people (even adults) lack confidence, they may not feel comfortable trying to do new things, take on challenges, or speak up for themselves. Does this describe you?

In *Being Me,* you'll get a chance to really think about what being confident means to you. And while you read this book, you will have some time to think about what will make you feel better about yourself.

Once you know what would make you feel better, it becomes easier to work toward it. As you work to try new things, you can gain confidence from knowing that you are taking risks to build up skills, make friends, or try new experiences.

There are many ways to increase your confidence, but there are also a whole bunch of ways that you might be keeping yourself from feeling confident. You'll learn about some ways that you might be sabotaging, or messing up, your chances to feel confident, and ways that you can work toward gaining confidence.

Changing your thoughts from negative to positive, learning to act confident, becoming your own best friend, and setting comfortable goals for yourself are some tools that you will read about as you go through the book. You'll read about other kids who have boosted their own confidence levels, too. You should know that while many young people have shared their thoughts and experiences with me, those thoughts and experiences remain private and confidential. All the examples in this book are not about specific kids. Instead, I have drawn from what I have learned from kids and created examples that will represent just the same kind of things you might be thinking and experiencing. I hope by sharing these examples (which are conglomerations or composites), you can pick up some tips for raising your own self-esteem and confidence.

Since confidence involves feeling comfortable with who you are right now, we will take time to talk about how to do this. There is also a kind of confidence that involves being comfortable with other people. Let's call this social confidence. We'll also take time to talk about how to stand up for yourself with other kids, how to start talking with others, the rules that sometimes apply to being in a group, and how to deal with other kids who may not treat you too well.

You may hope that when you become more confident, you'll always feel sure of yourself, in all situations, and that you will be happy all the time. The truth is that no one always feels confident. No one is always happy. Don't give up hope. Everyone (yes, that includes you!) can work toward feeling more confident, feeling better about themselves, being more accepted by others, and feeling happier. Isn't it time to put yourself in control of being you, the more confident you?

Ready to begin building your confidence? You've already taken the first step by reading this introduction. Think about asking your mom, dad, or another adult that you trust to read along with you. The information in this book can lead to really interesting discussions and other people can be a great support as you work toward increasing your confidence. You don't have to do this on your own!

Part one

Know
About
Confidence

Chapter 1

What Really Is Confidence?

So you want to build up your confidence. That's a great goal! But what exactly is confidence? Lots of kids struggle to define it. And it's hard for kids (and adults) to gain more confidence if they're not sure what it is. In this chapter, you will learn about confidence and how kids explain what it feels like to have it.

Recognize Confidence

Do you know people who have a lot of confidence? Close your eyes and take a minute to picture them. What words would you use to describe these confident folks?

Which of the kids below sound confident to you?

* the popular quarterback on the football team
* the straight A student
* the C student who's won a few drawing contests
* the student with okay grades who volunteers at an animal shelter
* the kid who gets A's and B's in school, has two close friends, and loves hip-hop

Tough decision, huh? It could be all these kids—or none at all. Why is that? Well, confidence isn't determined by what you do. It's determined by how you feel. Hank, a popular quarterback, might seem like he has lots of confidence, but he always feels like he just gets lucky in games when he plays well. Hank says, "I'm always worried that I'll mess up in the next game and no one will like me anymore."

In general, confidence can be defined in any or all of the following ways:

* You usually believe in yourself and like who you are.
* You believe that you can handle challenging situations, either by using your own problem-solving skills or by asking for help.
* You can laugh at yourself when you make mistakes and you work to correct them, without feeling bad about yourself.

Basically, confidence doesn't mean that you are better than anybody else, but that you are okay with being you. It also means that you don't need to knock down other people (physically or verbally) in order to

How would you define confidence?

feel good about yourself. Confident kids can compliment other people *and* still feel good about themselves. Confident kids can also admit to needing help at times, and to having both strengths (abilities) and weaknesses (areas that they are not yet super good at).

You may like these ways of explaining confidence, or you might want to stick with your own definition. There's no one right answer here. Many kids include words like "self-esteem," "comfortable," and "happy" in their definitions.

Do you beat yourself up when you make a mistake? Do you tell yourself that you're stupid or a bad person or just not good enough?

Afraid of Mistakes?

What happens when you try really hard but you make a mistake? The million dollar question here is: Can kids feel good about themselves, even though they're not perfect and sometimes make really noticeable mistakes? What do you think?

Well, human beings make mistakes. It's just a fact of life. Even the most confident person has likely made a bunch of mistakes. The important thing, and you've probably heard this tons of times already, is that you learn from your mistakes. And that you don't get down on yourself for them. If you need to work on making fewer mistakes, you can still feel good about yourself in the process because you're working to improve yourself (we'll talk about this a lot more in Part 2).

Mary loved to read and easily read the words in the books that her teacher picked for all the students to read in class. But when it was Mary's turn to read aloud, she started sweating, felt nervous, and excused herself to go to the bathroom. Mary said, "I was afraid of looking stupid. It would have been so bad if I made a mistake. I couldn't take that chance."

Mary's self-doubts kept her from showing her reading skills, an area that she had worked on. Teddy *did* read in class, and even though he knew how to read the words, he mispronounced one of them. Another kid corrected him. Teddy said, "I thought it was actually funny that I misread the word. It wasn't even a big word. It was no big deal, though. And so what! I know I'll never mess up on that same word again. And, I'm cool with me, so I'm cool with knowing that I'm not perfect."

How would you have handled this situation? If Mary felt self-confident, do you think she would have handled the situation differently?

Do You Believe in Yourself?

Everyone has a few areas that they struggle with, whether it's a sport, organizational skills, a school subject, or another area. Some kids find it hard to talk to other kids, make friends, or may feel uncomfortable in any kind of social situation. It can be really frustrating when you focus on what is hard for you and forget to spend time focusing on what you can do and what is special about you.

Cassandra's List

Cassandra was able to make a list of the problems she was getting into because of her thinking (or negative self-talk). Here is her list:

* I forgot that I do have special qualities. I'm nice and funny and a good listener.
* I was only focusing on my area of weakness, my shyness.
* I really knew that not all kids were super outgoing or had tons of friends, but I kept thinking that I was the only one who wasn't popular.
* Trashing myself took the pressure off me. I didn't have to try hard to make friends because I thought that no one liked me, so trying would be a waste of time.
* I was starting to think my whole life was useless just because I was shy.

Cassandra's change of thinking didn't happen overnight. It took time for her to really begin to believe in herself.

Can you think of ways you think about yourself that might cause problems?

What's Your Comfort Zone?

Have you ever heard the expression "being out of your comfort zone"? It just means that you're doing something that isn't very comfortable for you. When you grow from being a little kid to a tween to a preteen and then a teenager, you may notice that you feel less comfortable during these times of change. Or when you try something new or something scary, like giving a report in class when you're shy or running for a spot on the student government when you're new to a school. Change and new things can bring a sense of excitement and make your daily life very interesting, but it can also make you somewhat uncomfortable. Staying in your comfort zone may be safe, but you may also miss out on the great things that changing and taking healthy risks can lead to for you.

Bradley never wanted to try a new sport or group activity because he thought he wouldn't do well. He explained, "I was afraid other kids would think I was pathetic. I had that fear a lot."

Bradley talked to an adult who helped him to focus on his strengths and to question the reality of his fears. Bradley later said, "I knew that none of my friends automatically became amazing at a sport until they practiced, so why did I think I had to be perfect right from the start? I told myself that I'm brave to try new things, that I have things I'm already good at, and that I don't want to miss out on doing cool stuff just because I'm sometimes a little out of my comfort zone."

With a little practice, Bradley was able to handle a challenging situation and ask for help. He took small steps to build confidence.

Different Kinds of Confidence

There are two main kinds of confidence that we'll talk about:

* Self-Confidence (comfort with who you are inside)
* Social Confidence (comfort with the people around you)

Let's take a look at both of these, what they are, and see how they're connected.

How would you describe a confident person?

Self-Confidence

Self-confidence is a great starting point for gaining confidence in areas that involve people and things outside of you. How do you think about yourself? Do you feel proud of your achievements? Do you compliment yourself by saying things like, "Wow, my watercolor painting isn't bad for a first try"?

Self-confidence is about having faith in yourself. This faith does not come from handling every situation on your own. Actually, it comes from knowing what you can handle and when to ask for help. When you feel good about how you handled the situations, you can begin to feel more confident.

Self-confidence comes from accepting yourself, flaws and all! You can remind yourself that you may try new things and not succeed immediately, and you may even make mistakes. But if you put in the effort, can shrug off the mistakes that come with learning new skills, and smile when you succeed, you may just find that you feel good about who you are and feel more confident.

Confident kids feel good about themselves. They don't usually get too down when they can't learn something super quickly. They know that there are things that they are good at, so they keep trying to learn new skills. Self-confidence can show up when a person is learning anything, include learning how to kick a soccer ball, ice skate, sing, dance, and even how to do math problems. Confident kids are less likely to throw up their hands and say, "I'm just stupid. I can't learn this!" Giving up makes it hard to learn, and you don't get that amazing feeling of being able to say, "It was hard, but I kept trying!"

Social Confidence

When you feel that you like yourself, it will be easier for you to gain the confidence to socialize (hang out) with others. If you like you, why shouldn't others? The tricky part about socializing is that you can't control the other person. Some people might understand you or even like you more than other people do. The hard thing is to remember that other people don't give you faith in yourself or feelings of self-worth. That comes from inside you.

You don't have to have social confidence to start to take social risks. You can try speaking up for yourself, even if you feel that others might disagree with you. Nine-year-old Daniel did just that. Daniel's class was going to plan a dance for the entire school. Daniel went to a planning meeting and said that he thought a luau theme might be really fun. Most kids ended up voting for a country-western dance theme. But a few kids told Daniel that they would definitely think about his suggestion for a luau for a future school event. How do you think Daniel felt about this? Actually, he was glad that he had the confidence to give his opinion and that he had some kids thinking about his idea for another school dance or activity.

Social confidence involves how you feel when you meet new people. It shows up in the way you introduce yourself. It also includes how you talk to boys and girls, and how you act when you go to parties and dances. These experiences can create some discomfort. You may be out of your comfort zone. But trying these experiences and realizing that you got through them (and had some fun) makes you feel more confident today and more comfortable for future times when you are in those situations.

If you like you, why shouldn't others?

Do you need to feel good about yourself in order to gain social confidence? Or do you need to be successful socially and have social confidence to feel good about yourself?

The Confidence Cycle

Do you think that you need to feel good about yourself in order to gain social confidence? Or do you think you need to be successful socially and have social confidence in order to feel good about yourself?

Actually, the two kinds of confidence that we discussed (self-confidence and social confidence) interact and can have a big effect on each other. Take a look at the three circles above to see how it works. Basically, it's a cycle.

But if you don't have internal confidence (you don't believe in yourself), it's hard to gain social confidence. Social confidence can help to bolster your self-confidence, but it all starts with believing in yourself.

The Truth

If you're hoping to always feel amazingly self-assured or confident, then you should know that it's pretty unlikely. Most, maybe all, kids feel insecure or uncertain at times (and that goes for adults, too!). This isn't necessarily bad. For one thing, it's part of being a person. New situations and new people tend to make many kids feel a little uncertain or a little lacking in confidence. Also, sometimes feeling insecure or uncertain can be a cue that you're doing something new and exciting.

If you talk to the most popular kid in your class for the first time, you might feel a little unsure and nervous. But you can learn to deal with these situations so that you *seem* confident, even if you don't really feel this way (don't worry—we'll talk about this soon). Remember also that if you ever feel super nervous and uncertain, your lack of confidence can be your way of reminding yourself that you may not be ready for the experiences and that you may need guidance or help. No one feels confident about everything they try to do. But you can still feel good about who you are, while learning and asking for help.

I n this chapter, you learned how to recognize and define confidence. Self-confidence is all about valuing yourself and having faith in yourself. Social confidence has to do with how you feel when you talk to or socialize with others. Remember that confidence doesn't come from being perfect or being liked by everyone. It comes from knowing that you like yourself and can handle situations around you, either on your own or by having the comfort to ask for help.

Confidence Boosters

* I want more confidence and I'm willing to work for it.
* Even confident people sometimes make mistakes.
* I can start acting as if I'm confident, so I get used to what it feels like.

Chapter 2

Look out, It's Sabotage!

Do you know what sabotage is? It means an *intentional* act of destruction—that is, somebody messes up something on purpose. Now, what does this have to do with confidence? Well, *self-sabotage* is something you do to yourself when you feel you don't deserve good things to happen to you. Or you get into bad habits that work against you and you don't ask for help. You may not even realize you need help. Self-doubts are when you always question things about yourself in a way that robs you of confidence.

Why do we need to talk about this? Learning about these confidence killers (or ways you sabotage yourself) gives you the power to avoid them. Knowledge is power, and knowing how to break through what's holding you back will let you start feeling confident. The power lies with you. You have the power to make yourself feel more confident.

To start, here are some of the things kids do to sabotage themselves and keep themselves from gaining confidence. Ask yourself, am I:

* Beating myself up?
* Playing it too safe?
* Expecting perfection?
* Comparing myself to everyone else?
* Competing too much?
* Catastrophizing?
* Struggling with social fears?
* Having too much anxiety?

As you read about each of the confidence killers, you may want to keep your laptop or a piece of paper near you. If you think that you might have any of these problems, write it down. The rest of the book will help you gain the tools to stop sabotaging yourself and start building your confidence.

Beating Myself Up

Words are powerful and can really affect how you feel, think, and act. Words like *can't* and *won't*, and phrases like *I'm such a geek* or *I'm an idiot* can only make you lose confidence. These kinds of words and statements that you say in your head are called negative self-talk.

Do you have a little voice in your head that says, "I always make a fool of myself" or "Other kids always know what to say. I never do"?

Negative self-talk is when you try to convince yourself that everyone else is better than you, or that you're stupid, or that no one could possibly like you at all, or that you will do something that you will regret *forever*. If negative self-talk is playing in your head, you're sabotaging yourself. The danger is that if you say and think these thoughts over and over, you'll probably come to believe them.

One reason why kids use negative self-talk is that saying that they are a nerd or weird may actually feel safe. Safe? Really? Think about it. If you already insult yourself, you won't be so surprised if other kids put you down. They'll just have proven you right. What's more, you may, without even knowing it, think that it is risky to call yourself anything else but a nerd or stupid or weird because that would get your hopes raised. If someone insults you when you are more hopeful about yourself, it might hurt even more because you have more to lose. So, sabotaging yourself might be a way to protect yourself from leaving the safety of your comfort zone. But it robs you of confidence.

Brian's Story

Brian always felt embarrassed because, as he said, "I'm such a loser." When asked more about this, Brian explained, "I make mistakes a lot. Really dumb mistakes, like showing up to my friend's party before it was supposed to happen. I was 1 week early! That was so embarrassing. How can I ever get to be confident when I do stuff like that?"

Should Brian be embarrassed because he showed up for the party on the wrong day? Most kids would be uncomfortable in that situation, but a different kid might have just laughed at his (or her) mistake, apologized to the friend, and then decided to become more organized.

Have you ever made a mistake and then had the confidence to learn from it? How would you have felt if you were Brian?

Playing It Too Safe

Speaking of your comfort zone, never leaving or even stretching your comfort zone is called playing it safe. When you *risk* trying new things, you risk failing. Right? You might place expectations on yourself that you might not feel comfortable doing. So it may seem safer not trying anything new at all, but playing it safe won't pay off. That's because you won't feel the confidence that comes from trying. Confidence comes from taking the risk and leaving your comfort zone (with help, if you need it) without knowing if you will succeed.

In life, there are good and bad risks. A bad risk is one where there is danger, like taking drugs or skiing on the black diamond trail when you should be on the bunny slope. Taking a bad risk will probably not lead to confidence, but it may lead to illness, broken bones, and other really bad consequences. Healthy risks, on the other hand, are ones that are safe and help you grow as a person (as corny as this sounds). Trying to succeed is something worth being proud of. Not trying doesn't give you a chance to succeed.

Expecting Perfection

You may watch other kids do things and think that they are always perfect. Well, guess what? Nobody's perfect. And the few people who come close to perfection don't get there without putting in a lot (a lot!) of effort. Many famous authors actually were rejected when they first tried to get one of their books published. Imagine if J.K. Rowling gave up! You should always work to do well and enjoy what you are doing without being unrealistic in expecting to magically get something right the first time or for you to always perform perfectly.

You are probably perfect at some things, like saying the word "the" or putting on your clothes in the right way (underwear first, pants second). If small things like these are all that you take pride in, life can be very dull. When you risk leaving your comfort zone and trying something a bit more complicated or challenging, you can expect to make mistakes. Don't pressure yourself to be perfect. You can remind yourself that you will probably make mistakes and that it's okay. Some of your mistakes might even be funny, and being able to laugh at yourself is a big part of becoming confident.

Comparing Yourself to Others

Do you have a brother or sister who seems to excel at a lot of things? Do you sometimes dream of being just like another kid in your class?

If you compare yourself to others, there is a real danger. You may fall into the trap of feeling less important, less talented, and less competent. What you may really be saying to yourself is that your own abilities aren't as worthwhile as the other person's.

It's okay to admire other people for their talents. But if you try to force yourself to think like, act like, and be like another person, then you are not being true to you.

Being unique doesn't mean worse. It means special. Real confidence comes from being happy with who you are, not how well you copy someone else's ways. Sometimes it may take the help of a teacher, a coach, a parent, or another person you know to introduce you to an activity that you will do really well in.

Competing Too Much

Kind of related to making comparisons is being involved in competition. There are two kinds of competition. The first one is when you

Stop Beating Yourself Up!

Margo used to really get down on herself when she made mistakes. Then she learned to catch herself. Here's what she does now:

* I calm myself down so I can think more clearly.
* I remind myself that everybody makes mistakes, so it's okay for me to mess up sometimes, too. And I can even learn from my mistakes.
* I practiced how I'd handle making a mistake. I just roll my eyes and say, "Oh well."
* I asked my friends to call me out if I start getting down on myself.

Can you come up with your own ways to stop kicking yourself for a simple mistake?

compete against others, like when you want to be first seat in the saxophone section of the school band and you have to compete against other kids for the spot. This form of competition can be very healthy, but only if it motivates you and doesn't discourage you. The other kind of competition is when you compete against yourself. This is when you challenge yourself to do better at something than you had before. Just remember to be realistic. If you got 98% correct on a math test, be wary about expecting a higher grade.

Catastrophizing

Have you ever heard of the phrase "making a mountain out of a molehill"? That's catastrophizing. It is when you make a small problem into a tremendously serious obstacle. If you're on a hike, a small pebble on the ground is not a problem. You just walk right over it. If you run into a large boulder blocking your path on your hike, it is a tremendously serious obstacle. And you need to rethink continuing on that path. When you look at a small pebble and treat it like it's a large boulder, that's catastrophizing.

Have you ever catastrophized? Have you ever said something like "I didn't say that vocab word right in Spanish class. I'll never learn Spanish!"? That would be taking a small mistake and making it into a tremendous problem.

Struggling With Social Fears

If you have convinced yourself that other kids won't like you, then your low confidence level may lead you to avoid socializing. Or maybe you're really shy about talking to boys or girls and you think you'll just look stupid if you try. Try using positive self-talk to fight the negative

Annie's Story

Annie practiced soccer for hours each day during the weekend. She was on a travel team and wanted to beat last year's championship team. Annie knew that the other team was tough to beat. She wanted to do her best to help her team. So she practiced and practiced. The competition motivated her. When her team later lost to the other team by just one goal, Annie still felt good. She didn't like losing, but she felt that she helped her team to get close to winning. This competition, then, was healthy for her.

Have you ever been in a situation like this? How would you have reacted if you were Annie?

self-talk and self-doubts in your head. Remind yourself that you are worth getting to know. Give it a try. Pick one or two kids to start talking to about things they're interested in. If certain kids don't warmly welcome you, it's their loss. Pick others. Think of it as an adventure—you won't learn how well you can do in social situations if you don't try.

Having Too Much Anxiety

Did you know that having a little anxiety when you're stretching your comfort zone is a good thing? It's true. It helps you to pay attention to more details, so you can focus on carefully balancing on your ice skates when it's not automatic yet, or it keeps you alert when you are taking a test. On the other hand, too much anxiety can make life stressful and you may feel too scared to try new things. Here are some tips to reduce nervousness:

* Remind yourself that it's okay to feel a little nervous.
* Tell yourself that excitement and anxiety feel the same in your body, so you may be excited about a new challenge.
* Focus on your strengths.
* Remember that it's okay to make mistakes.
* Take slow, deep breaths to calm your body.
* Count backward from 100 by tens.
* Seek out help if the anxiety is interfering with building your confidence.

Did you know that having a little anxiety when you're stretching your comfort zone is a good thing?

One really fun strategy is to use your five senses (vision, hearing, smell, taste, touch) to relax your mind and your body. Katrina said, "I tried this and it was fun. I pictured being at the beach, seeing the waves, hearing the seagulls, tasting and smelling the salty ocean air, and feeling the touch of the sand between my toes. It was hard to stay nervous before my recital when I had this in my head and when I remembered that I wouldn't die from being nervous."

Even though anxiety is a large blocker to building confidence, it's only briefly being mentioned here. So if this is your major blocker, talk to the adults you trust and see if you can get help from them or from a professional trained to help kids get rid of excess anxiety. You don't need to suffer alone. It's a sign of strength to know when to get help.

There may be ways that you sabotage your chances to gain confidence, but there are ways to avoid these obstacles. Beating yourself up, playing it too safe, expecting perfection, comparing yourself to others, trying to be just like another person rather than just like you, unrewarding competitions, catastrophizing, withdrawing socially due to fears, and having too much anxiety can all be obstacles.

In the next sections, we'll talk about what you can do to boost your self-confidence and how to begin to feel more comfortable when you deal with school and friends.

Confidence Boosters

* I will stop beating myself up when I make mistakes.
* I will take the time to give myself pep talks.
* I will compliment myself.
* I will remember that confidence comes from inside me.

Part two

It's All About You

Chapter 3
Know Yourself

Do you know yourself and what makes you special? Do you value yourself? If you don't know and value those special qualities that make you you, then you end up depending entirely on other kids or adults to build up your confidence. Confidence starts inside you, with knowing and accepting (and liking!) who you are.

In this chapter, you'll get a chance to know yourself better by looking at:

* Your strengths and weaknesses
* Your comfort zone
* How you're changing

Know Your Strengths and Weaknesses

Do you know yourself and what makes you special?

Focusing on your strengths can help you feel good about yourself. You can also use your strengths to gain the confidence to address your weaknesses.

If you believe that you can only gain confidence once you get rid of weaknesses, hold it right there. Everyone has at least one area of weakness. It could be someone's fear of public speaking, or their lack of patience with learning new things. You may not want to focus on a weakness, but it's good to know what it is. You gain confidence from working on what challenges you most. Let's take a look at how you can start this process.

What is on your list?

One helpful way to see what your strengths (things that you're good at doing and your special qualities) are and to figure out your areas of weakness is to make a list. Sometimes kids focus so much on what they need to improve that it can be a relief to spend time focusing on what they do best. Look at the list of qualities and activities on page 30. Use it as a jumping off point to make your own list of strengths and weaknesses.

Since the list on the next page isn't an absolutely complete list, you may find that you have strengths that aren't on the list. Make sure you add them to *your* list. When you're finished, share your list with your mom, dad, or other adult who knows you really well. Let them look over your list of strengths to see if they think you left anything out.

As you already learned, expecting to be a superstar is a nice idea, but liking yourself for who you already are (and maybe expecting to be better at something tomorrow than you are today), is truly what can build confidence. Accepting yourself, even though you're not perfect, is the first step toward building confidence.

baking * cooking * drawing * painting * art * pottery *
photography * sewing * singing * lacrosse * skiing *
playing a musical instrument * fishing * golf * dancing *
gymnastics * football * soccer * tennis * ice skating *
fencing * surfing * baseball * organization * responsibility *
honesty * sharing * nonjudgmental * good under pressure *
funny * being a good friend * altruism * creative * reading *
speaking in front of others * math * writing * history *
spelling * handwriting * vocabulary * geography * astronomy *
pop-culture trivia * shopping * fashion * stamp collecting *
robotics * recycling * model airplanes * gardening *
coin collecting * good with animals

Now, look at your list of strengths and weaknesses. See if you can use them to build your confidence. Look at the list to remind yourself that you have special qualities and strengths. Focus on the positive, while working on the areas you want to improve.

Here's what you can do to feel more confident in being you:

* Use your list as a way to give yourself a pep talk when you're down. ("I may have some things I want to change or improve, but I have strengths, too.")

* Write yourself a letter. It doesn't have to be more than a few sentences, but it should include a lot about your strengths and

Tony's List of Strengths and Weaknesses

Strengths	Weaknesses
Making people laugh	I get embarrassed easily
People can count on me	I can't draw in art class
I take care of my dog	I get mad too quickly
Most of the time I'm honest	I get low science grades

Come up with your own list of strengths and weaknesses. What's on your list?

unique qualities. Even if it feels silly, once you finish this letter, read it again and again to remind yourself of the positive ways you act, feel, and think.

* Keep adding to your list. See how it grows and changes over time.

Your Comfort Zone

So, what's your comfort zone? Where and when do you feel safe? Is talking to your best friend in your comfort zone, but not talking to new kids? Think about it. Your comfort zone can expand if you take time to work at it. When your comfort zone grows, so can your confidence!

> **What's your comfort zone? Where and when do you feel safe?**

Finding your comfort zone is important because that is generally the place you feel safest. If you want to stretch your comfort zone, it can be helpful to move gradually from it. That doesn't mean trying out for the football team even though it scares you when someone throws a ball in your direction in PE class. It doesn't mean going away to summer camp when you are nervous spending 1 night at a friend's home for ev thought that he wasn't good at anything, especially sports. Later Zev said, "I found out that I have a whole bunch of things that I'm good at. I am a decent painter, I play the piano so-so, I am a good speller, I'm honest. I'm a really good friend, and I care about people. And I'm into recycling to save the planet."

Once Zev began to focus on his strengths, his confidence in himself grew. He discovered that he even had the courage to ask a friend to teach him how to play tennis.

Have you ever avoided a new situation because it was outside of your comfort zone? If so, what did Zev's example show you? How can focusing on your strengths help you to stretch your comfort zone?

a sleepover. What it does mean is taking a small step, a step where you are not too upset or nervous, in the direction that you want to go in. So if you like hanging out with a friend, see if he'll have a sleepover with you at your house. Once you are used to this, you can think about sleeping at his house.

Sometimes kids try to stretch their comfort zone so far that they become super scared and upset. Then they might even give up trying. Taking small steps seems to be more comfortable for kids and they are less likely to give up.

Understand How You're Changing

Just when you learned to be an infant, you changed into a toddler. When you learned how to be a toddler, you changed into being a young child. Now you are changing again. Not only is your mind changing, but your body may be changing, too.

Brianna always wanted to take ice skating lessons but she was shy. She got super nervous whenever she thought about meeting a coach and taking the lessons. She was in her comfort zone whenever she was with her friends and a few close cousins. She asked them if they wanted to take lessons with her. It turns out that one of her cousins was interested and the two of them signed up. Brianna used her knowledge about her comfort zone (feeling good with her cousin) to figure out how to do something outside of her comfort zone. Could you think of something you could do to stretch your comfort zone? Can you think of someone who can help you?

* You may become insecure about how your body looks.
* You may question your clothing style.
* You may wonder if a boy or girl you like will like you back.
* You may also begin to wonder about whether you can handle the responsibilities of getting older.

Yikes! Well, you are not alone! Every kid your age is going through these changes. This is why the tween, preteen, and teen years can be challenging but also so interesting. Some changes can be filled with excitement but may also include some uncertainty. You may notice that you are feeling different than you used to when you were younger. Maybe you are feeling more confident or less confident right now.

What about you? Are you ready to move forward by stretching your comfort zone slowly?

Your comfort zone may also change. You may suddenly want to take on new roles, like running for the student government, or you may suddenly find that you are more nervous about doing things that you used to be fine with. When Peter was 11, he began thinking about what his future would be like in 10 and 20 years. He wasn't sure if he was ready for high school tests and getting a job. The idea of getting married scared him. He was so upset about all these

33

worries that he no longer felt comfortable around many of his friends, since he imagined that they had it all figured out. Just because other kids don't always talk about their feelings about changing, doesn't mean they don't notice it and think about it. Peter's older brother talked to him about the changing expectations. Peter realized that he's only a year older than a 10-year-old and should just work on being 11, not 21 or 31.

If you want to expand your comfort zone, focus on today and tomorrow. It makes it easier to deal with the changes and your increased goals without feeling overwhelmed.

It's important to focus on your strengths to build confidence, but confidence also comes from working to improve areas that are difficult for you. You read about your comfort zone and how you can start to stretch it by doing things that are just a little outside of this zone. This chapter also covered the fact that you are changing, and this can be fun, scary, or both. You can't stop it. You will soon be a teenager, then later an adult. Remember that these changes don't happen overnight and that you can get help to cope with these changes. In the next chapter, you'll read more about how to get support during stressful times.

Confidence Boosters

* I will focus on my strengths.
* I will recognize my weaknesses and ask for help if I need it.
* I will compliment myself on working hard.
* Overcoming fears and difficulties will help me to feel more confident.

Chapter 4

Get Through the Tough Stuff!

Even when you're feeling pretty confident, you will run into problems and tough times. This happens to everyone, even the most self-assured people.

There are a lot of ways to get through the tough stuff and challenging situations. Here are a few ways that we'll talk about in this chapter:

* Use your support team
* Deal with teasing
* Handle disappointments
* Laugh with yourself

Use Your Support Team

If you are having trouble focusing on the positive things about yourself, it's definitely time to talk to someone you trust. Let someone else help you to stop letting negative self-talk mess with your head. If you fell down and needed stitches, you would want help and wouldn't hesitate to get it. If your feelings are down you may also want help, and it's a good thing to ask for it if you are having difficulty managing on your own.

Do you think that you need to handle everything on your own in order to feel confident?

Remember that you don't have to go through life alone! Build your support team, your cheerleaders, people who know and care about you.

Everyone's support team looks different, so make sure yours reflects you and your needs. Here's who might be on your support team:

* Your parents
* Your teachers and coaches
* Your siblings and friends
* Other trusted people

Let's take a look at who these people are and how they can help you.

Talk With Your Parents

Your parents have an important job. Their job is to help guide you and help you feel good about yourself as you mature and face challenges. Talking with your mom or dad (or both) can be a super decision. You may have heard this before, and it's true—your parents were once your age. They were once kids and they had to grow up, just like you. Parents can be a sounding board with whom you share your feelings, concerns, and needs. Most kids put their parents at the top of their support team member list. How about you? It can feel really good knowing your parents have your back. If you feel that you can't talk with your parents, have you figured out why? It might help to sit down with your parents and find a way to talk with them about this.

Lean on Teachers or Coaches

Once you know what is upsetting you, you can build your support team. If it's about schoolwork, wouldn't you want to add a teacher? Maybe you can see the teacher for extra help. If you are worried about how to handle a situation, who else can you ask in school? Here's who you could ask:

* Coach
* School social worker
* Teacher
* Guidance counselor
* Principal

Emily's Talking Tips

Emily has some ideas for when you talk to your parents. These ideas helped her!

* Tell them how you feel about yourself. I didn't feel like I really fit in with the other kids in school.
* Tell them about what you're good at and what's hard for you. I'm great at science and math and stuff, but I have a hard time talking to other kids.
* Let them know what you think they can do to help. I said they could help me practice talking in front of my class.
* Tell them you need them to be on your support team. My parents didn't know I needed their help until I told them. I realized they aren't mind readers after all!

Pick the people you trust and then let them know that you want to talk. It could be helpful to schedule an appointment so they can really take the time to listen.

Hang With Your Siblings and Friends

If you are worried about how to handle a situation, who can you ask in school?

Are you one of those kids who feels insecure and goes home after school to your room and closes the door? Kids who do this may feel alone, lonely, and different. Does this describe you? One of the best ways to help yourself feel less alone is to be with other people. If you have a brother or sister, or good friends, who are trustworthy and can give you pep talks, hang with them.

Do you feel insecure and go home after school to your room and close the door?

If you try to hang out with a group of kids who you think are popular, but that you don't really talk with, you may feel lonely even when you are around them. Standing near people is better than being in your room alone, but talking with them can help you feel included in what's going on around you. Find kids who you enjoy being with and have fun with!

Talk to Other People

Often, professionals (like a psychologist) see hundreds, or even thousands, of kids and are experts on what can help kids feel better. Sometimes, kids think that they have to be "crazy" to see a therapist. When people seek help from a therapist, it's a sign of health not of "craziness." These kids and adults care about themselves enough to want to feel better. Not seeking help when you're in emotional pain and can't seem to feel better on your own is probably not the best choice. Therapists will let you know that it is a sign of courage, not a sign of weakness, to walk through their doors and into their offices.

There are so many other people around you who might be able to join your support team. People such as cousins, aunts, uncles, grandparents, neighbors, or religious advisors could talk to you when you need to talk.

You probably know a lot of people. Of course, you don't want to talk to people who could make you feel bad, who you know won't give you positive advice, or who can't be trusted. Whenever you feel like you need help to feel better or to handle a tough time, try to think of at least four people who could help you. You may only need one or two of them, but have extra people, just in case. If you know that you can turn to people for support, you may not feel as alone, and may find that you feel more confident to take on challenges since you have a team of supporters behind you!

Deal With Teasing

Yes, being teased stinks. It's hard to feel good about yourself when kids keep teasing you. Teasing and bullying are big topics that can take up a whole book to talk about. But for this book, let's just say that those other kids may like to tease you because they have anger issues, they know that they make you feel bad, they get a reaction from you, or they get a reaction from other kids who watch as they are teasing you.

If you really feel good about who you are, kids teasing you might annoy you, but would probably not keep you from being confident. Remember that confidence comes from how you feel about you.

Here are some ways you can deal with being teased:

* Ignore it. They may get bored with teasing you if you don't seem to care about what they say.
* Hang with a group. It's harder to tease you if you have a group of kids who support you nearby.
* Use positive self-talk. Remind yourself of your strengths, so the teasing doesn't bring you down too much.
* Tell the person teasing you that you don't think it's cool. Sometimes the other person is just getting carried away with joking in a way that really isn't funny and can be hurtful.
* Seek out your support team, including some adults, for guidance. See if they have other suggestions on how to handle being teased by the kid or kids. And at times, adults may need to step in and talk with the other person in order to make the teasing stop.
* Stop trying to be friends with a kid who is always teasing you. Friends are supposed to make you feel good.
* Regain your power and make changes only if you want to make yourself feel good!
* If you feel that you are being bullied (physically or verbally), then it is time to talk with your support team members to figure out the best way to deal with it.

Handle Disappointments

You probably don't like having disappointments, such as failing at something. But if this happens, how can you learn to accept and learn from these situations? It's just like what you already learned about learning from your mistakes—you can learn from disappointments and failures. If negative self-talk takes over, then it's hard to really grow from these experiences.

ean used positive self-talk after he didn't get a trophy at a chess competition. He told himself, "I learned a new move from the guy who beat me and I can't wait to use it. I tried my best and got better from being in the competition. I was brave to compete and I have more confidence in me now that I tried." What could you say to learn from a disappointment, without losing your confidence?

Laugh With Yourself

Sometimes you, like everyone, may get so wrapped up in things that you take everything too seriously, including yourself. Step back and look at the situation. Did you accidentally call your teacher "Mom" in class? Yes, it's embarrassing, but isn't it also a little funny? Laugh with yourself. Did you drop your tray in the middle of the crowded cafeteria at lunch? The room got silent, everyone stared at you, and laughed, right? Well, think about this—would you have laughed if you saw someone on TV do that? If the answer is yes, then you can laugh with yourself. Remember, no one is perfect.

If you can laugh with yourself when you make a mistake, you can have more fun. If you can laugh with yourself, you'll also probably feel less pressured and more motivated to take a risk and expand your comfort zone. If you can laugh with yourself, you are probably going to start to feel more confident. When you laugh with yourself, you *look* more confident to the outside world, so this might help you to actually *feel* more confident. You'll also remember that whatever mistake

Isn't it also a little funny?

Would you have laughed if you saw someone on TV do that?

41

* I am not alone in this world.
* It's a sign of strength to know when to ask for help.
* I have people in my life who value me and whom I can trust and talk with.
* If I laugh with myself, mistakes may not seem so bad.
* I have ways to handle being teased now!

you made probably wasn't catastrophic. The world didn't end, right? You didn't hurt anyone. You can laugh, relax, and move on!

You are not alone, and it is a sign of strength to know when you need to call upon your support team. You can choose who is on your support team, but just make sure that the people build you up, point out your strengths, and that you trust their opinions and suggestions. Now that you know who might be on a kid's support team, you can start picking your own team members. You learned that disappointments, and even failures, do not have to crush your self-confidence and that laughing with yourself can sometimes take the pressure off of you when you do make a mistake. Now you have ways to cope with teasing and disappointments.

In this chapter, you thought about ways that you can gain support from others to feel good. In the next chapter, you will learn about ways that you can use positive self-talk to build up your confidence.

Chapter 5
Change Your Thoughts

Changing how you think about yourself is not the final step in making you more confident, but it's a really good place to start. Words and thoughts can change your feelings and actions because your mind is extremely powerful. The self-talk you do in your own head, the talking to yourself, can help or hurt you. The way you think about yourself can help or hurt you. In this chapter, we're going to talk about how you can help yourself with your words and your thoughts.

?

When was
the last time that
you took time to
give yourself a
pep talk?

Positive Self-Talk

Like you've probably already guessed, positive self-talk is your running internal pep talk. It's the encouraging thoughts and good things you say to yourself to keep you, well, positive. Positive self-talk can give you the courage you need to expand your comfort zone. It can keep you from feeling really frustrated and beating yourself up when you make a mistake. It can remind you of why you should feel good about you.

Instead of using the negative words that make you feel bad about yourself, try switching to positive words. Change all those "I'm so stupid!" thoughts into something more positive, something that is friendlier to you. This takes a lot of practice, so hang in there. It'll take some time for you to get used to changing your self-talk. The first step is to know the words that make you feel bad about yourself and the ones that make you feel good. This helps you keep a positive mental attitude.

Positive Mental Attitude

What is a positive mental attitude? It's when you focus on what you can do well and also know that you are capable of building up areas of weakness. A negative mental attitude is when you convince yourself that you will probably fail at things, even before you try, or that you're just not "good enough". If you often say "I know I won't be able to do it" before you try a new activity or project, you probably need work on your mental attitude.

A positive mental attitude keeps you from going negative and getting down on yourself. When you think positively, you focus on the bright side. If you say "I think I can" (remember that train?), then you are more likely to give the new adventure a really enthusiastic try!

Positive Thought Continuum

If you use positive self-talk to give yourself encouragement, it will be easier to feel good about yourself and to have a positive mental attitude. If you have a positive mental attitude, then it's easier to feel good and give yourself pep talks when you need them. These two factors feed off each other! It's like a cycle or feedback loop.

Watch out, though, since the same goes for negative self-talk. It can lead you to feeling discouraged and having a negative mental attitude, which can lead you to more negative self-talk. Even if you aren't comfortable with it yet, try using positive self-talk and focusing on having a positive mental attitude. You might just find that you feel better about yourself, that you feel more confident!

How does having a positive mental attitude affect you?

Are you an expert on negative self-talk? How can you break through this negativity?

Stay Positive About You

There are a lot of things you can do to keep the pep talks and positive thoughts coming. We're going to go over how to:

* Change your words
* Create positive scripts
* Visualize good things happening
* Compliment yourself

Change Your Words

Getting rid of the words that keep you from feeling good about yourself is one of the most important things you can do to build your confidence. Remember that how you think has a really strong effect on how you feel and on what you try to do. Try catching your catastrophizing statements or thoughts, smile or laugh at how exaggerated they really are, then replace them with more realistic comments.

You can change *I can't* into *I can try*. You can change *I won't*, like in *I won't be able to do it,* into *I can try to do it*. Give yourself a chance to succeed. Don't shut the door to learning and challenges!

Create Positive Scripts

Think of something that you might not feel confident about doing. Are you worried about a math test that's coming up or are you nervous about signing up for summer camp?

Audrey's Sample Pep Talks!

Here are some pep talks that Audrey uses when she is feeling down. Try them while you're coming up with your own!

* Yeah, I'm different than other kids. I don't want to be an exact copy of someone else. I'm unique! That means special. That means cool!
* I don't have to be totally amazing at any one thing. I'm good at a bunch of things.
* My friends like me, so I know I'm likeable. That makes me feel better.

You can also check your list of strengths when you're not feeling too good about yourself. What are all the wonderful things that make you you?

What are you thinking? What is your self-talk? Can you change any negative statements you might be telling yourself into positive ones?

It may feel kind of weird at first when you try to use positive self-talk. But give it a try. You may want to pretend that you are writing a movie script for someone going through the same situation as you. What would you want the confident, courageous person in the movie to think and say? Maybe those lines would be good for you, too. Elizabeth said, "I told myself that I don't have to be perfect to be great. I said that I can handle new things on my own or by asking for help. I feel more confident now that I focus on the positive stuff."

What are you thinking? What is your self-talk? Can you change any negative statements you might be telling yourself into positive ones?

Visualize Good Things Happening

If you believe in yourself and can imagine yourself succeeding, it will help you to try new things in your life. For instance, do you want to ask another kid in class if he wants to work with you on a social studies project? Are you too nervous to ask since he may say no? Picture success. Picture yourself going up to him and casually asking if he already has a partner for the project. Imagine him saying that he does not. Next, imagine asking him if he wants to work with you and him saying yes.

Now, what's another way this situation could go? Picture that. Does he laugh at you? If so, this is clearly a negative image. Now try making it positive. Imagine him saying okay or politely explaining that he already has a partner. Either way, you visualized asking him to work with you. Congratulations! Confidence comes from challenging yourself, trying new things, and reminding yourself that you are worth knowing!

Ethan's Story

Ethan liked to read about American history. He knew a lot about it and loved to talk to his parents about history. He thought about joining the History Club at school. They read books and talked all about history.

Ethan finally told himself, "I might really like the club. So what if kids don't agree with something I say. They might like what I say, though. I'll never know unless I try. It might even be fun!" With this pep talk, Ethan began to feel better about taking the risk to join the club. He went to a meeting and came home feeling really happy.

Do you have something you want to do but are afraid to take the risk? What kind of positive self-talk could you use to psych yourself up to try it?

Of course, not all of our hopes and wishes automatically come true by imagining that they will. But you are in control of whether you take a risk and how you react if something doesn't go your way. Visualizing good things happening is helpful, but visualizing how you would handle things if they don't work out as planned is just as important. Try practicing smiling and shrugging your shoulders at the same time. You can remind yourself, "I tried. That's what counts." You can still feel good about you, even when things don't work out the way you planned.

Do you get mad at yourself because you focus on the errors that you made?

Compliment Yourself

You'll read about the importance of complimenting yourself several times in this book. If you study for a test and get an 87, do you compliment yourself on the fact that you studied hard and got many of the questions correct? Or do you get mad at yourself because you focus on the errors that you made?

You are the only person who will be with you everywhere you go in life. So be a good friend to yourself. Pat yourself on the back when you work hard, make efforts to try new activities, and work to expand your comfort zone!

Now you should be familiar with positive and negative self-talk and how your self-talk and mental attitude can take you a long way toward feeling good about yourself and feeling more confident. You learned about some ways to focus on the positive, such as changing your words, creating positive scripts, picturing success, learning from others, and complimenting yourself.

In the next chapter, you'll learn about a pretty advanced kind of self-talk. It's when you convince yourself that you can act the way you want to be, like act confident even before you feel it. Let's give it a try—you might even have fun!

Confidence Boosters

* Focusing on the positive can make me feel better.
* If I picture being confident, I can gain the courage to do new things!

Chapter 6

Act As If

So you're shy. Try acting as if you are a really outgoing person.
Why would acting like you're more confident than you are help
you feel more confident? Good question. It's actually a simple answer,
though. Pretending that you already are the way you want to be gives you
a chance to see how it feels. It also lets you practice what skills you need
in order to become more confident in general or in a certain situation.
Practice helps you learn in school, so why not practice when it comes to
learning how to feel better about yourself?

Here are some techniques that we'll discuss in this chapter:

* Imagine it
* Plan what you'll say
* Role play
* Watch your body language
* Use positive self-talk

Imagine It

Before you can act as if, you need to know what the situation is and what you want, that will lead you to feel better about yourself and more confident. So, the first thing to do is to imagine what you want. Imagine *how* you want to be. Close your eyes. Think about how you can feel more confident in a situation. Eddie, for example, said, "For the first time in my life, I let myself actually think about talking to the cool kids on my basketball team. They're the most popular kids in my grade. I imagined talking to them and feeling good."

Now it's your turn. You don't have to worry about how you will get to truly feeling confident. Right now, just get there in your mind. Experience how great it feels. Feel what it will be like to be more confident. Does it feel good to you? If so, you may notice that you're standing taller and even smiling in your imagination when you practice feeling confident.

Hold on to this image. Also, remember that the good feelings can be there in real life when you act as if, using your imagination to guide you. If you can imagine being self-confident, then you know that it is worth working on becoming that confident person you imagined.

Plan What You'll Say

If you are trying to act as if in a situation that involves other people (kids or adults), try to take a few minutes to figure out what you might say. Some kids think that they should just be able to walk up to another person and say the perfect thing. Remember, no one is perfect, and there's no such thing as the perfect thing to say. Also, if you are trying to say something, or talk to someone, and you are

Tina Knows When to Act As If

Should you act as if whenever you're facing something scary or overwhelming? Actually, the answer is no. Here are some times when Tina acts as if:

* Giving a speech that she worked on for class
* Going to a dance with friends
* Taking a test that she studied for but is nervous about taking

Here are some times when she doesn't act as if:

* Taking a test when she never studied for it
* Doing something that she really doesn't know how to do
* Doing something dangerous that she was dared to do

feeling nervous, being prepared with what to say can be a great help. You can:

* Rehearse;
* Change what you want to say;
* Practice it;
* Say it.

Hold on to the positive self-talk and positive mental attitude that you learned about in Chapter 5 when trying to figure out what words to use here. Gregory decided not to think negatively, like saying to his teacher, "I know I'm not so smart, but can you help me anyway?" In his imagination, he used the words, "I'm trying hard and get some of this math, but can you help me understand it better?"

Maybe you want to go to a school dance, but you are shy. In your head, try planning what you might say to some other kids at the dance. If you plan it and imagine it, it is easier for you to do it!

Role Play

Once you can imagine what it would be like if you act as if you have confidence and you plan what words you could use as you act confident, it's time to role play the situation. There are many ways you can do this.

Practice alone. You can just sit in your room and act out the role, the way you would if you were already confident. Think about your tone of voice and whether you sound nervous or confident. Also, pay attention to how loud or soft you speak. It's hard to seem confident when you mumble or speak really softly. And, take notice of your body language.

People pick up on these things (maybe you can try picking up on them when you're around other people, too). You can even think about the place where you'd like to feel confident—school, the basketball court, the mall, you name it.

Talk to yourself in the mirror. Watch yourself as you do this. If you met the person you see in the mirror, would you think that kid was already confident? If not, what's wrong with the picture? Once you figure that out, you can change it. If you think the person in the mirror is acting confident, then you're on your way to actually being confident!

Sometimes, kids may not be sure if they seem confident. Are there people around you who could role play with you and give you feedback? What about a parent? Your grandparent? An older brother or sister or cousin? They may have some great tips for you, and it can be fun!

If you met the person you see in the mirror, would you think that kid was already confident?

Are there people around you who could role play with you and give you feedback?

Katie was invited to a sleepover birthday party for Sophie, who was super popular. Katie felt that her invitation must have been a pity invitation. "You know, I was invited because Sophie felt sorry for me but really didn't want me to go."

Katie talked to her dad and he helped her to act as if she were confident. Katie imagined getting a warm, happy greeting at the door by her friend and she practiced what topics to talk about if she needed something to say.

Katie was nervous the morning of the party, but she went. All her practice worked! Katie went home feeling better about herself and more confident. She faced her fears and was able to take on a challenge outside of her comfort zone! How would you have handled this?

Watch Your Body Language

While you're role playing, look at your body language. This communicates as much as your words do. Someone who is not confident often has trouble making eye contact. Here's what you can work on to have more confident body language:

* Make good eye contact. Of course, that doesn't mean you have to stare at the person constantly.
* Try to relax your shoulders.
* Smile when you're talking about something fun or when you're trying to be friendly.
* Try not to fidget too much.

Can you do that? Sometimes it takes practice. That's where the role playing becomes so useful.

Use Positive Self-Talk

This is a reminder to use positive self-talk when you imagine yourself acting as if you have confidence. Give yourself a pep talk before trying to decide what words to use in your role play. What can you tell yourself? Are your words positive? If you act as if you're confident and feel good about yourself, other people will usually notice this. If you show that you like you, others may now want to know more about you, too!

A cting as if you are confident can help you practice how it will feel to actually be confident. You learned some techniques for practicing being confident, like imagining it, using positive self-talk, role playing, picking words that you would use if you were confident, and working on confident body language. If you practice being confident, it becomes a bit easier to actually go into a situation where you are unsure or nervous and to seem more confident. If you seem more confident, you will likely feel better about the way you managed the situation, which can lead to truly increased confidence!

Now that you have learned about how to act as if you are more confident, and you know that you can imagine handling new situations, it's time to turn to the next chapter and learn about how to gradually increase your comfort zone without feeling overwhelmed.

What can you tell yourself? Are your words positive?

Confidence Boosters

* Acting as if lets me practice being the way I want to be.
* If I act like I like me, other people may want to know me, too.
* My words and body language are important for showing that I'm acting confident.

Chapter 7

E X P A N D Your Comfort Zone

Taking healthy risks and leaving your comfort zone can be scary. You may feel nervous because you might not know what to expect. Things might be different and *you* might become different as you try new things. Remember in Chapter 2, when you learned that playing it safe can keep you from gaining confidence? In this chapter, we'll talk about ways that you can expand your comfort zone and begin to feel more confident because you did this.

You'll learn about how to:

* Be brave
* Be ready for bumps in the road
* Go at your own pace and take small steps
* Ask for help

Be Brave

Accepting that you might be nervous as you leave your comfort zone is a huge step. You need to have courage, you need to be brave, to do it. If you think that other kids don't get nervous when they start to change, think again! They may not always show that they are anxious, but that doesn't mean that every challenge they attempt makes them 100% comfortable. It might be helpful to talk with a parent or someone else on your support team about this. They've probably been nervous at times in their own lives.

Before you start to challenge yourself and take some risks, do some positive self-talk to convince yourself that it's time to take steps outside of your comfort zone. This can give you the courage and motivation you need.

Be Ready for Bumps in the Road

You might be asking yourself, if taking risks is so scary, why bother? And that's a good question. Lots of kids don't take risks, even if they're healthy risks, because they're sure they'll fail at anything they try. They convince themselves that they can't do well. And guess what? A lot of the time it's not trying that leads to risks. It's true!

Not trying can make you feel safe at the moment. If you don't try, you can pretend that you could have been the best if you had tried. But not trying can lead to problems. Not taking risks, not expanding your comfort zone, probably won't make you feel good or confident. Actually, it might make you feel sad, because you'll miss out on the fun that other kids are having while doing new stuff.

If you are willing to give yourself a chance, you open the door to succeeding. Once you try, you can be proud of that attempt. Once you feel proud, you will likely feel more confident. Even if you don't succeed at first, trying is something to feel good about.

As you try new things and take chances, you will probably make some mistakes while you expand your comfort zone. That's normal! As you take risks, remember:

* If you don't expect yourself to be perfect, then hopefully you can feel less anxious about how you will handle the new experience.
* Give yourself a pep talk if you start to feel unsure. You can tell yourself that trying something takes courage and can lead to confidence.

Not trying or becoming too upset when things don't go perfectly can lead to frustration and lower confidence. Let's talk about how to move forward and take the risk to expand your comfort zone.

Beat Your Nervousness!

When you go out of your comfort zone, you might get a little nervous. Here is what you can do:

* Take a slow deep breath in, then slowly let it out. Do that three times.
* Exercise to get rid of that extra energy.
* Visualize a calming story or picture.
* Think positive thoughts.
* Count backward from 20 by twos.

You can make a list of what works for you.
Do you know of other ways that you calm down?

Go at Your Own Pace and Take Small Steps

If you're trying to expand your comfort zone, you may feel a little uncomfortable. It's something new and a little bit of discomfort is expected. Hopefully, you also feel a little bit of excitement. You may want to rush through the experience, trying to take huge steps so you can gain confidence quickly. This is not like a relay race in PE class.

Instead, give yourself time to figure out what pace is right for you. It's okay to take small steps and go at your own speed.

Baby steps aren't just for babies! If you take one small step, then another, and later another, you will have made steady progress at your own pace without feeling overwhelmed.

It's like climbing a ladder. If you set up the ladder near where you want to go, then walk up the first step, then try another step, and another, and another, you'll make it to the top. If you are afraid of heights, you may hang out on the first step for a while. But you made the first move toward expanding your comfort zone! Later, you can try the second step. After you get used to that, you can go for the next step. Remember, you can make it to the top of the ladder if you take baby steps. And always compliment yourself after each step!

Ask for Help

Have you noticed that there have been several places in this book where you read about how asking for help can be a positive thing? Well, it is! Adults do it all the time. Confident kids also do it—they

Have you ever felt frustrated and disappointed when you have tried to build up your confidence in the past?

How can you get help when you need it?

Do you have a good friend who you can buddy up with?

Kristine's Baby Steps

Taking small steps can let you feel more comfortable.
Here are some things to try to help you prepare for
your steps:

* Look at your list of strengths and remind yourself that you're
  a great kid already.
* Get rid of the negative self-talk.
* Find a team member to work with you to expand your comfort zone.
* See what happens if you smile three times each day for the next week,
  while you tell yourself what you like about you.
* Act like you already have confidence.
* Remind yourself that you are not in competition with others. You just need
  to like yourself and work to be the best you that you can be.
* Set realistic goals for yourself so you don't get overwhelmed or discouraged.

How do they sound? Will they work for you?

may go into school early to get extra help from the teacher, or call a
buddy to get help with a homework assignment that confuses them,
or even find themselves crying and talking with a parent about a
fear they have about trying something new and possibly not
doing well at it.

Do you remember the many ways you can ask for help?
How can you get help when you need it?

Tara's Story

Tara was 9 and she wanted to take art classes at her community center. She said, "I didn't know anybody and I was too scared to go alone. My mom and I set up a ladder with baby steps."

At first, Tara and her mother just walked there and looked around. Tara got comfortable with the outside of the place. The next step was that she and her mom went into the community center where the class was going to be held. They got papers about the class and went on a tour of the building. Next, they went back and asked the teacher if her mom could sit somewhere in the place while Tara took the class. Tara took two classes while her mom sat and read a book in the next room. After that, Tara knew a few kids in the class, she liked her teacher, and she felt comfortable having her mom wait outside in the car. It wasn't until the last day of the class (7 weeks later), that Tara was okay with her mom dropping her off and coming back to pick her up later. "But I made it! I did it! I feel so much more confident now! I was so nervous but I still was able to do it! Now I love my art class!"

Tara set up her steps and moved forward. Because of this, Tara gained confidence. How would you have felt if you were Tara after the first one or two steps? How would you have felt if you were Tara after 7 weeks of taking the class? Try not to become impatient as you take small steps forward. Taking small steps might just give you the confidence to take future steps!

Do new things with your friends. Lots of kids find it is easier to try new stuff, or show their special qualities, if they know that they have another person there to support them. Do you have a good friend who you can buddy up with? Hannah said that it was easier to try out for the school play when she knew that her BFF was going to try out, too.

At times, you may find that you and a friend both want to do something new, but neither of you have enough information to help the other. This is okay. You can learn together. Many friends find it more fun doing something new with someone else. You can share your frustrations, laugh at your mistakes, and cheer each other on.

Talk to your number one supporters. If you've kept your fears bottled up inside, try talking to someone on your support team. Remember, if you listed these people as supporters, it means that you trust that they will support you and not make you uncomfortable when you talk to them. They'll accept your weaknesses, challenges, and concerns, then guide you.

Stick up for yourself. Yep, this is part of getting help, too. If you find that one of the people you turned to for support ends up pressuring you to change too quickly, stick up for yourself and say that you're uncomfortable. You can teach that person about how taking small steps forward, as long as you're moving forward, will still help you to take on healthy risks and that that is what you want them to support you on.

Confidence Boosters

* I will remember that taking small steps is okay!
* I'll give myself a break when I don't get something right the first...or third time.
* It's okay to be nervous.
* I can turn to my supporters to guide me and help me to expand my comfort zone.

You can work at your own pace as you try new activities or experiences. Remember that baby steps are not only for babies. If you're not overwhelmed, you can move forward more easily, so pick steps forward that feel right to you. A little discomfort is normal, too much means that you are trying to move forward too quickly. Remember that moving forward is like moving up the ladder—taking one step at a time can get you to your goal! You can compliment yourself for each step, asking for help along the way when it will help you to move forward, and you do not have to do something perfectly in order to feel more confident.

In the next chapter, we'll talk about ways that you can reward yourself for your accomplishments and be a part of a support team to help other people. Helping others can often make kids feel even better about themselves.

Chapter 8

Be Your Own Best Friend

Being your own best friend means caring *for* yourself! This means that you don't just like yourself, but it means that you take time to take care of and work on valuing yourself.

In this chapter, you'll get a chance to focus on you and the ways that you can appreciate and take care of yourself. We'll talk about how you can:

* Appreciate and reward yourself
* Spend time with yourself
* Improve your talents
* Work on being healthy, inside and out
* Help others

Appreciate and Reward Yourself

You might think that rewards and getting a toy or a video-game are the same thing. But there are really great rewards that don't require money or your parents for you to get. You can reward yourself all by yourself. You can:

* Compliment yourself.
* Pat yourself on the back and say, "Nice job!"
* Make a list of your goals and put giant check marks next to those items that you accomplished.
* Smile when you think about being you.
* Tell someone close to you about something that you are really proud of doing.

As you already know, building confidence can be tricky, especially if you don't feel confident about yourself at all right now. You can start to build confidence by taking the time to appreciate yourself.

Have you ever rewarded yourself? What did you do? What will you do now?

Spend Time With Yourself

This seems obvious—you're always with yourself. You can't leave yourself to go somewhere else. So why learn about how to spend time with yourself? Actually, many kids keep so busy with school, with after-school activities, and with family time that the only chance they have to think about being alone with themselves is just before bedtime. By that time, it's probably late and you're probably tired.

It can be fun to schedule Me Time. Have you heard of Me Time? Any idea what you do during this time?

Have you heard of Me Time?

What could you do for your Me Time?

Tom's Tips for Appreciating Yourself

There are lots of ways to appreciate yourself. Here are
a few suggestions that Tom thinks work!

* Set aside some time to be by yourself. Plan what you're
  going to do.
* Do something goofy, like writing a fun song about yourself or making
  up a dance. You don't have to share it with anyone else,
  or you might want to. Just focus on having fun doing it.
* Feel good when you help others. Maybe raise money for a dog rescue
  place or donate your old clothes to a charity where other
  kids could use them.

Me Time means finding ways to enjoy being by yourself. If you have a
friend over to hang out, you probably have certain things that you like to
do. What about when the friend isn't there? Some kids like to draw.
listen to music, or collect baseball cards. How do you spend your time?

What could you do for your Me Time? Think about whether you want
to do something more with this time to enjoy being with you. Try to
remember that you can be your own best friend and enjoy spending
time with just you.

Improve Your Talents

While it is true that confidence often comes from working hard to
accomplish or overcome something, sometimes it's important for you
to stop and take time to be proud of those special qualities that you
already have. What is easy for you may not be easy for others. You can

work to build on these talents to get even more skill and more pride! If you have talent that comes easily to you, work at it to do the best you can. You can feel confidence in your natural abilities and the way you work to develop them.

If you find that you have a particular area of talent, whether others share it or not, you can feel confident that you found an area of strength.

Denise was good at sewing. She'd been doing it since she was little and learned by watching her grandmother sew. She used her Me Time to sew small outfits for her stuffed animals. But she never thought much about her sewing skills. One day, Denise decided to ask her grandmother to help her learn to make a skirt. Denise suddenly felt brave, since she was willing to learn something new. She enjoyed learning and she felt more confident once she realized that she was gaining an area of talent that she had not had before. Now she was learning to make clothes for people!

How about you? Once you find your area of strength, why not build on it? Remember that you don't have to become the best in the world, just work toward becoming the best you can be.

Work on Being Healthy, Inside and Out

Taking care of yourself means working to have a positive mental attitude and appreciating yourself. It also includes taking care of your body. Sometimes kids forget about this part of being good to themselves. What about you?

What is on your list of strengths?

Once you find your area of strength, why not build on it?

Here are just a few ways that you can check if you are taking care of yourself:

* Do you eat regular, healthy meals?
* Do you get enough exercise each day?
* Do you smile?
* Do you spend enough time outdoors?
* Do you take care of your body with good hygiene?

Can you add to the list? How do you show that you are taking care of yourself?

Help Others

Did you know that you can actually build your own self-confidence by helping others? Sounds odd, but it's true. Knowing that you've made a difference in someone's life can help you feel good about yourself and it will remind you that it's okay for you to get help, too.

Did you know that you can actually build your own self-confidence by helping others?

Helping another person is probably one of the easiest (and best) ways to feel useful and valuable. You can help someone else to feel more confident, less alone, less scared, or more cared about. Wow!

Focusing on others is helpful when it is altruistic. Altruism means that you help other people because it feels like it is the right thing to do, not because you hope to get invited to a cool party afterwards or because someone will pay you for doing something nice. The world needs kids who care about and help others. Is this you? If it is, then add this to your list of talents or strengths and build on it. Feel confident that you have this special quality.

Eli's Ideas for Helping Out

You may want to know what a kid can do to really make a difference. Here are a few ideas that Eli has for helping out:

* Walk your neighbor's dog just for the fun of it.
* Surprise your younger sister and let her listen to a song on your iPod.
* Leave your parents a note thanking them for something kind that they did for you.
* Do an extra chore around the house without anyone asking.
* Compliment another kid in school about an answer given in class.
* Sit with a lonely kid at lunch.

Be creative and make up your own list of possible altruistic acts. It's fun to see the happiness that another person can gain from your caring behavior. Also, focusing on helping other people often can decrease a kid's discomfort with being around other people. Is there a way that you can help out others and feel more confident because you are the type of person who cares?

It's important to take time to appreciate and value yourself. You can reward yourself when you feel that you have expanded your comfort zone or used positive self-talk. You read about how you can use Me Time to learn how you can enjoy being with yourself, even when no one else is around. Also, the importance of building on your talents, working on being healthy, and helping others were reviewed. In the next chapter, you'll read about ways to build up your confidence while you are at school.

Confidence Boosters

* I can enjoy Me Time.
* Helping others is a special quality that I have!
* I will take care of myself, inside and out.

Chapter 9

Be Cool With School

There are many kids who sometimes feel unsure when they are in school. Are you one of these kids?

To build your confidence in school, the most important thing is that you work to do *your* best, not to *be the best*.

So how do you do your best in school? Here's what you can do to build up your confidence and do your best:

* Stop procrastinating
* Get organized
* Participate in class
* Get help when you need it
* Don't try to be perfect
* Congratulate yourself on small steps

Stop Procrastinating

Procrastination is when you wait until the last minute to do something, like studying for a big test or doing your science project.

Why do kids procrastinate? A big reason is that putting off studying or practicing also means putting off the pressure that studying or practicing may create. Studying might make you really anxious when you feel confused or overwhelmed by the subject. Not studying can give you some relief since you temporarily avoid the pressure. You might even think, "Why bother? I'm going to fail anyway." If you think like this, then you've given up before even starting.

Here are some tips on how you can stop procrastinating:

* Ask an adult, like a teacher or a parent, for help getting started.
* Set up a schedule where you do small, quick steps over time, rather than facing the stress of doing a large chunk of work at once.
* Remind yourself that doing things step-by-step can move you forward and it can feel good to move forward.
* Remind yourself that you don't have to finish everything in one night if you start preparing early.

Do you procrastinate? If you do, then what are some ways that you can do it less and, soon, even stop procrastinating?

Get Organized

Organization has a lot to do with feeling confident in school. It can help you feel like you're really in control of your schoolwork. If you organize your studying and start studying early, you can take small easy-to-manage steps each night toward learning even the stuff that's a little hard for you.

Here are some hints for getting organized:

* Guess how many hours it will take you to do something. Then figure out how long you want to work on it each night. If you need one hour to write an essay for school and you have six days left, you can work on it only 10 minutes a day and still get it done on time. Not so bad, right?
* Get a calendar and write down the dates of tests and when projects are due, so you don't have to keep track of everything in your head.
* Set up project schedules for long-term assignments, showing what you will do each day or each week.

Once you find the techniques that work for you, you may find that you feel more confident that you can organize yourself and get your schoolwork done.

Do you know how to become organized?

Participate in Class

Are you uncomfortable speaking up in class? Do you sit quietly, not sure of what to do or say?

You might think that you can only participate in class once you feel confident in yourself. But that's not completely true. Participating in class (when you're not super confident) can actually build your confidence. By speaking up in class, you get to ask questions and get answers to those questions. Also, speaking up lets you share your ideas and, sometimes, add an entirely new idea or thought into the class discussion. Other kids may even wish that they had your confidence to speak up!

Jack's Project Schedule

Here's Jack's schedule for finishing his science project on gravity:

SATURDAY: Figure out what the project will be and list the different parts I'll need to do.

SUNDAY: Read the gravity section in my science book.

MONDAY: Research gravity online and at the library.

TUESDAY: Create an outline for my paper.

WEDNESDAY: Write the hypothesis section of my paper and come up with the details for my experiment.

THURSDAY: Conduct my experiment.

SATURDAY: Write the results section of my paper.

SUNDAY: Write a draft of my final paper.

MONDAY: Show the draft of my paper to my teacher and ask if I should add anything to the project.

TUESDAY: Make corrections on the draft and finish the paper.

WEDNESDAY: Hand in the paper.

Here are some tips you might want to try until you are ready to speak up in class:

* Ask your questions or share your ideas with your teacher before or after class.
* E-mail your teacher your questions if that's easier for you and okay with your teacher.
* Ask a friend a question you might have about the class. You can even do this casually in study hall or in the hallway if it's a quick question.

Asking questions and getting used to participating in class can help you to feel more comfortable about talking. Try it out. When you're more comfortable, your confidence can grow!

Get Help When You Need It

Knowing that you can turn to others for support when you need it can help you to feel more confident. You can try to do homework on a new math concept or study for a Spanish vocab quiz on your own, but get help before you get too frustrated.

Here are some hints for asking for help:

* If you don't understand something immediately, take a deep breath, remind yourself that you don't have to get it the first time around, and then try it again.

School Pep Talk!

Give yourself a pep talk to feel more confident about speaking up in class. Here are some things that Amy says to herself:

* I won't die from talking. I might just enjoy it.
* Even if I don't answer a question right, I'll know that I tried. And I can feel confident that I was brave enough to try.
* If I don't ask questions, they might never get asked and then I won't get my answers.
* Even if kids laugh at something I say in class, or call me a name like a nerd or even a geek, I can just smile or even try to laugh.

Can you come up with your own pep talk for when you want to speak up in class?

* If you still don't understand, ask a question that is exactly what you want to know.
* Remember that you know a lot of stuff already! Think about the subjects you do really well in or know a lot about.
* Know that asking for help isn't a sign of weakness.

Don't Try to Be Perfect

The truth is that no one is perfect. Remember reading about this earlier in the book? Have you ever met a baseball player who always hits home runs? Unlikely!

Here are a few ways to help you steer clear of the need for perfection:

* Learn from your mistakes. You don't have to like making mistakes, but you should remember that some of the best learning comes from trying, making a mistake, and learning how to correct it.
* Work to do better than you have done in the past, but don't focus on being the best or being perfect. If nothing else, it takes the fun out of the adventure.

Always trying to be perfect can leave you feeling unsure and upset. Try thinking of what you can say to yourself, when you are not perfect, so that you can feel confident in yourself and proud of your accomplishments.

What do you do when you struggle to learn something?

Do you want to be perfect? Do you want to get straight A's in all of your classes?

Do you imagine that you will be confident once you're perfect?

Congratulate Yourself

Each small victory is something to be proud of. And congratulating yourself can help build your confidence!

Here are some ways you can congratulate yourself:

* Put a big check mark next to each homework assignment that you finished.
* Remind yourself that getting started is a big step, so you can feel good about beginning your work.

Do you encourage others to do their best and compliment them when they do a good job? Don't forget to do the same things for yourself. Can you think of ways to congratulate yourself?

Procrastinating and trying to be perfect can lead to frustration. That's the bad news. The good news is that once you start getting organized, participating in class, knowing that it is okay to ask for help, and focusing on your strengths, you are likely to find that you feel more confident in school! Once you feel confidence within yourself, you are ready to move to the next section about feeling confident with others.

Confidence Boosters

* Trying for perfection can equal frustration. Trying my best can equal confidence!
* I can ask for help so I can learn new skills.
* Each small step forward moves me closer to understanding my work and to feeling more confident in school.

Part three

It's all About
You...and
Other People

Chapter 10

Stand Up for Yourself

Standing up for yourself can be scary at first since you may need to take a risk when you voice your feelings, beliefs, and needs. But standing up for yourself can actually lead you to feel more confident, even if you don't feel really confident right now.

How can you begin to stand up for yourself? There are lots of ways to stand up for yourself. Here's what we'll talk about in this Chapter so you can work on this skill and gain confidence from doing it:

* Standing up to your friends
* Asserting yourself with your parents
* Asserting yourself with other people

The Basics of Standing Up

Here are some tips that Elyse uses when she stands up for herself:

* Be careful not to sound aggressive or harsh. Starting your sentence with the word "you" can sound aggressive, like saying, "You have to change my bedtime" or "You are so unfair."
* Start a sentence with the word "I". Say, "I feel that..."
* Show respect, so no name calling or put-downs. Thank the listener for taking time for you.
* In your body language, show that you are serious but not confrontational. If you find yourself laughing because you are nervous, just explain this to the person. Also, try not to cross your arms.
* Invite the other person to ask you questions so that he or she really understands what you are saying.

Standing Up to Your Friends

Most kids don't really like confronting their friends, but sometimes they know that they need to stand up for themselves and let their friends know how they feel. Do you ever want to say something to a friend but are afraid of what the reaction will be?

So when should you stand up for yourself and let others know what you are feeling or thinking? If you feel pressured by a friend to do something you don't want to do, then you might want to stand up and voice your opinion. Is your friend pressuring you to drop another friend? Let her copy your test paper? What can you say? How can you keep the friendship but still feel comfortable?

Stand Up to Your Friends

Here are things that Jimmy has said to his friends:

* It's awesome that you like baseball. It's not my thing, though. How about if we do something else together?
* I am not really friends with Stephanie, but she's okay. I feel a little uncomfortable when you tease her. How about if we give her a break, okay?
* I feel funny saying this, but I don't want to let you copy my test paper. It would feel weird to do that. How about if we become study buddies, so you learn the stuff yourself?
* You're a really cool friend, but we don't have to agree on everything, right?
* I'm not saying your idea is wrong for you, but it doesn't feel right for me.

Can you think of other things you could say?

Asserting Yourself With Your Parents

Parents aren't mind readers. If you have a question or worry, they may not always know just because you thought it or just by the way you act. It can be hard to stand up for yourself and tell your parents what's on your mind but, most often, it's definitely worth it.

When you approach your parents, here are a few things you can do so you feel ready:

* Set up a family meeting time with them, so they can have the time to listen.
* Plan what you're going to say.
* Calm yourself by taking a few deep breaths before starting the conversation.
* Remember to be respectful when you discuss your feelings.
* Speak clearly and as calmly as you can.

Speaking Up to Your Parents

Here's what Tina has said to her parents:

* Mom, I don't get something. You never tell people about me being in skating competitions. Are you embarrassed by how I skate?
* Dad, I know you want me to do well in school. But you don't let me prove to you that I can stay up later and still do well in school. Can we talk about this?

If you plan what you're going to say like Tina did, you'll be better prepared to assert yourself with your parents.

* Be specific. Let them know exactly what you are thinking.
* Do not make accusations like "You're the worst dad. You don't love me."
* Give your parents time to respond or to schedule another meeting so they have time to think about what you have shared.

If you aren't sure if you can have this discussion, try role playing it with a sibling or with another trusted adult. Have you thought of what you want to say? Have you thought about how you want to say it?

Can you have a discussion with them about things that are important to you?

Asserting Yourself With Other People

Have you ever been waiting to ask a question in a store and the adults seem to ignore you? It happens to a lot of kids. How would you handle this situation? Would you walk away feeling bad? Would you speak up? If you feel strongly that it is important for you to be heard, how can you gain the confidence to stand up for yourself?

Here are a few things that you can do:

* Remind yourself that you are worth being heard.
* Try to imagine what you might say if a person is ignoring you or not taking what you're saying seriously.
* If you are nervous, try acting as if you are confident .
* Visualize yourself speaking up and then do what you did in your imagination.
* Speak up directly or ask an adult for help.
* Role play what you'd say and do.

Do you have more ways you can prepare to assert yourself with other people? If not, try getting suggestions from people on your support team. Remember, the more you stick up for yourself, the easier and more natural it will become.

How can you gain the confidence to stand up for yourself?

Knowing When to Ask For Help

Luckily, you don't live on this planet alone. Confident kids and adults know that sometimes it's important to get help. You may decide that you want to talk with a school counselor, ask your parent to help you with a social studies project, or ask your friend what suggestions he might have for starting a conversation with a new kid.

Do you always ask for help because you don't have confidence in your abilities? Do you always avoid asking for help because you think that asking for help is a sign that you lack confidence? Are you able to sometimes rely on yourself and sometimes turn to others? Having a balance in this area is important.

Margaret is a sixth grader. She always used to get high grades. She studied hard and felt confident in her ability to do schoolwork. But Margaret's English teacher, Mr. Chapman, was giving her much lower grades than she thought she deserved. So Margaret decided to stand up for herself.

Margaret told her older sister, "I think this guy hates me. I think I'm doing A work, but he keeps giving me B's. It's so annoying." Her sister reminded her not to accuse Mr. Chapman of anything and to try to be assertive not aggressive.

Margaret set up an appointment with Mr. Chapman. She took a deep breath to calm herself before they met. "Hi, Mr. Chapman. Thanks for seeing me." Margaret wanted to start the talk positively. "I wanted to talk about my grades. I'm confused. I study really hard, but I can't get the grades I used to get." Her heart was beating fast, but she felt good that she was standing up for herself.

Mr. Chapman said, "You have great ideas, Margaret. It's just that you don't check your spelling and I take off for that." Margaret never had points taken off for spelling before, but she admitted that she was sometimes careless in her spelling. "So, if I correct my spelling errors, what grades would I get?" Mr. Chapman smiled and said, "I think you would get top grades if you took more time to check your spelling."

At the end of the meeting, Mr. Chapman said that he should have been clearer in his comments on her papers and Margaret said that she was going to try harder to avoid careless spelling errors. Margaret felt more confident after standing up for herself!

Have you ever been in a situation like Margaret's? What would you have done if you were Margaret?

Standing up for yourself can help you to feel more confident and more comfortable with those around you. You may feel nervous doing this sometimes, but that's okay. When you stand up for yourself, you can feel better understood by those around you after you are heard. Now you have lots of ways to stand up for yourself and know that it's okay to ask for help when you need it. Now you are ready to take your newly found confidence and meet new kids!

Confidence Boosters

* I know how to stand up for myself and I deserve to be heard!
* My opinions are valuable and I want others to know about them.
* I can ask for help sometimes and rely on myself sometimes.

Chapter 11

MEET New Kids!

Have you ever started a conversation with a new kid in class? What about a kid you never spoke to before, or a kid you used to hang out with a long time ago but haven't talked with in a few years?

So how do you meet kids and make new friends? If you combine your positive self-talk and strategies for building confidence, you can meet kids and build your social confidence, too. It takes practice but you can do it. In this chapter, you will learn

* How to introduce yourself
* What to say and where
* What to say after the introduction
* How to use body language

How to Introduce Yourself

Let's talk about introducing yourself to other kids. Remember reading about baby steps? Taking small steps forward still moves you in a positive direction and allows you to stretch your comfort zone more easily. And when it comes to meeting new kids, sometimes small steps are even better than large steps.

Think about why you want to get to know that kid. Is it because he or she seems nice? Or is that kid always going to the NBA games in your city and you want to tag along? Maybe you want to meet this kid because he's popular or she's smart. Think about the reasons for wanting to hang out with this person. If someone hung out with you for the same reason, would you be happy about it?

Hopefully, you want to meet the other kid because of similar interests regarding her hobbies, sense of humor, or cultural background. So, the first step is to make sure that you want to meet the new kid for the right reasons. If you have a new kid in your class, you may want to get to know him because of curiosity and to make him feel welcome. These are great reasons.

What can you do if you have a low level of social confidence?

Make yourself comfortable. Now that you know why you want to meet a new kid, you are ready for this next step. If you're uncomfortable with other people, or afraid you'll say the wrong thing or be judged badly, meeting new people can feel uncomfortable and maybe even a little painful. What can you do if you have a low level of social confidence? Before even talking with the new kid, here are some tips for increasing your level of social comfort and confidence:

* Remind yourself that you are about to expand your comfort zone, so it's natural to feel a little uncomfortable.
* Give yourself a pep talk.
* Look over your list of strengths, since that is what you can share with the new kid.
* Calm down. Take deep breaths, visualize calming scenes, and do whatever you know relaxes you.
* If you are still nervous, act as if you have the confidence.

What are you going to say to introduce yourself?

What to Say and Where

You now know who you want to meet and why. It's time for a few more steps.

Where will you introduce yourself? If you want to say hello right after English class, but you only have a few minutes to quickly gather your books, walk down the hall, and get to your Social Studies classroom, this is probably not the best time to start a conversation. The bus may be a good place, but it is often packed with kids, noisy, and there can be a lot of distractions.

Think about the kid you want to get to know. What are you going to say to introduce yourself and where would you do this? Here's some steps you could try:

* Visualize yourself introducing yourself to a new person.
* Think about what you would like to talk about.
* Think about how you would start the conversation. It could just be a few short sentences.
* Practice saying what you want to say.

Tom's Opening Lines

Struggling to find that perfect thing to say when you
start talking to someone new? Well, there is no such
thing as the *perfect* opening line. Here are some lines that worked for Tom.

* Great field goal today!
* I love animals. I saw that you had a picture of a cat in your locker.
  Is the cat yours?
* I liked your drawings from art class. I draw cartoons. Who are your
  favorite artists?

**Think of your own opening lines. Use what you know about the other kid
to start a conversation. Got any ideas?**

What to Say After the Introduction

So, you practiced an opening line and delivered it. Congratulations!
You took on a challenge and can gain confidence from doing that.
After you introduce yourself, there are a few ways that kids can
respond—they can let you know that they don't want to hang out with
you right now or that they do want to get to know you better—and
there are different ways to respond to each.

Rejection

What if the other kid didn't respond well? Does this mean that you
lose confidence? Remember that no one can take confidence away
from you unless you let them. You can use positive self-talk by saying,
"I'm still special and a nice person. His loss. I'm glad to know that I
tried, and I'll keep trying because there are lots of people who will like
me." You can end the introduction, feeling proud of yourself.

If a kid doesn't seem to want to be your friend, there is no need to keep trying to develop that friendship right now. You may end up being friends in a few months, years, or not at all. If someone doesn't want to be your friend, it doesn't mean that the kid doesn't respect you. He may just feel that you are too different from one another.

Why would you want to hang out with a person who doesn't like you?

In some cases, though, she really may not like you. So why would you want to hang out with a person who doesn't like you? If you feel that you like you, then you can feel confident and keep looking for kids who click with you. You probably don't want to have hundreds of best friends anyway. Pick kids who like you and whom you feel good being around.

Acceptance

Now, what if the other kid seems to want to get to know you? Do you think, "Oh no! I didn't practice saying anything else"? Try not to panic. If you *really* listen to the new kid, she may give you hints on what you can ask her about. Is she talking about getting home to walk her dog? You can ask her about what kind of dog she has and what the dog's name is, right? If you don't know what to say, you can always ask about some of the following topics:

* What do you do for fun?
* Where did you go to school before moving here?
* What's your favorite subject?
* Are you going to the comedy night next week?
* Do you have any brothers or sisters?

Think about the place you met this person. You can probably find something about that place to talk about. Be creative!

Natasha's Story

Natasha was really shy. She was afraid that other kids might think that she's "dumb" or "weird" so she tried to avoid kids. She really wanted to meet new people, though. Finally, Natasha talked to her dad about this. He had a job where he had to talk with large groups of adults, so he was an expert on getting to know people. He told Natasha a big secret. He said, "When I start to talk, I remember that it's better for people to know something about me than to guess. If they like what I say, great. Even if they don't agree with me, they know a little bit more about me and I feel good that I tried to talk with them."

The next day in school, Natasha decided to let people know who she is. In the cafeteria line, Natasha's heart pounded and her hands felt sweaty. But her dad had said that this might happen if she got nervous and that it wouldn't kill her.

Natasha asked the girl in front of her, "Have you ever had the salad here? I'm thinking about getting it." The other girl turned toward her, seemed surprised that the question came from Natasha, and then began talking about how she didn't like the cafeteria food. Natasha agreed and they talked about the cafeteria the entire time they were on line. While Natasha didn't get invited to sit with the other girl, she still had a smile on her face for the rest of the day. Can you guess why Natasha kept smiling?

Natasha was smiling because she took a risk, even though she felt nervous saying something at first. "I went out of my comfort zone and I want to do it again. I feel more confident now!"

What could you do to begin a conversation with someone new? How do you think you'll feel once you do it?

How to Use Your Body Language

Now that you decided which kid you want to start talking to, and you know what words you will use to start the conversation, it's time to focus on your body language. As you already read, body language can communicate lots of information. When you're with other people, it can show whether you're really interested in the other person, whether you have self-confidence, and whether you are distracted.

Here are some tips on using positive body language:

* Make eye contact to show that you respect what the other person is saying.
* Smile when the person says something interesting or funny.
* Nod your head if you agree with or understand what the other kid is saying.
* Stand tall to show that you have confidence in yourself.
* Try not to cross your arms.

You can practice your body language by role playing getting to know someone new. Remember that you can practice by looking in the mirror or with someone from your support team.

It's a great idea to take small steps, over time, as you get to know someone else. There are many ways to start a conversation and continue it with someone you just met or with someone you really didn't know very well. Now that you know where to meet new kids, and how you can communicate through body language, you can take the next step and get to know them. In the next chapter, you will learn about how social confidence can help you learn to get to know and talk with boys and girls—those kids you might have a crush on.

Confidence Boosters

* I am worth getting to know!
* Other kids won't know if I'm interested in them unless I start a conversation.
* I can act as if I have social confidence as I meet new kids.
* I can gain confidence just by trying to expand my comfort zone and meeting new kids.

Chapter 12

Talk to Boys and Girls

Do you have a crush on a boy or girl yet? If not, believe it or not, you will probably experience it some day. It's all part of growing up.

In this chapter, you'll learn that you don't have to lose your confidence just because you have new feelings about boys or girls. Just like you learned earlier, there are ways to sabotage your confidence in this area and many ways to build confidence. Let's focus on the positive strategies.

You'll get a chance to read about:

* Understanding your nervousness
* Taking your time
* What to say to *that* person
* Self-talk
* What to expect

Understanding Your Nervousness

Trying to handle having a crush means expanding your comfort zone, so it's not surprising if you feel nervous. Do you feel your heart beating faster, your palms getting sweaty, or you can't think of anything to say when the kid you have the crush on is around? All of this really is normal and happens to other kids, too, so hang in there.

You may be thinking that you feel kind of uncomfortable and confused inside. Even if you feel a little nauseous around that person, it's normal. Your body and mind are reminding you that you are feeling and doing something new. If you focus too much on the nervousness, it can make the situation stressful. If you focus on the excitement, it can make your crush into a wonderful adventure. It can be exciting if you focus on the positive feelings! Soon we'll talk about how you can practice what to say to the other person and what to say to yourself to calm down.

If you feel nervous because your entire self-confidence is dependent upon this person liking you back, then we have a complication. Self-confidence comes from inside you, not from what this person can give you. Sure, it's great if the person likes you back (and maybe even a little scary, too!), but your value remains the same whether the person likes you or not. We'll talk more about this soon.

Do you feel your heart beating faster, your palms getting sweaty, or you can't think of anything to say when your crush is around?

Taking Your Time

Do you want to tell the other kid that you have a crush on him or her? Right now? Here's some advice: Don't rush the crush. The other kid may be scared by these new feelings that you have, even if the kid likes you back. Ina said,

Do you want to tell the other kid that you have a crush on him or her? Right now?

What do you think could have happened to their friendship? Would you have handled this situation differently than Ina?

"Max and I were friends since kindergarten, so when I started having a crush on him, I went right up to him and said that we should go out 'cause I like him. I thought that I was showing that I was confident and could just say what I thought." How do you think Max reacted?

Max always thought of Ina as one of his best friends. But Max could have thought, "I like Ina a lot. But this crush thing can wreck friendships. I've seen it. I don't know if I can deal with this right now. I think I'll ignore her for a while."

How do you think Ina would have felt if Max thought this and ignored her? What do you think could have happened to their friendship? Would you have handled this situation differently than Ina?

Take your time. You may not have had a crush on anybody a few months ago or a year ago. Things change. What you don't know is whether the other kid's feelings are the same as yours or if they'll change over time. Having confidence doesn't mean that you take a giant leap forward. It means that you feel that you can handle the new situation. Many times, handling it means taking small steps forward.

Here are some things you can do when you have a crush:

* Remind yourself that you are okay with you, even if the other person doesn't have a crush back on you.
* Take time to calm yourself, so you don't rush into doing or saying something.
* Think about how the other kid would feel about your crush.
* See if you can just get to know that person as a regular kid first.

* Talk to your really close friends and see what they think about your crush.
* Can you hang out with the kid in a group? This can be more comfortable for both of you.
* Try sitting with the kid at lunch or call that person to talk on the phone.

These ideas are ones that you have probably thought about before, when you just wanted to have more friends. The same rules apply right now. You can expand your comfort zone by including the kid you have a crush on in your circle of friends, but do it in small steps so you don't feel too nervous and you don't risk making the other kid feel nervous. Yes, other kids can feel nervous about this whole new experience, too!

What to Say to *That* Person

You know about role playing what you can say to new kids. You can role play what to say to someone you have a crush on, too. A lot of kids find that they struggle to talk to the kid they have a crush on, even when they've been friends or classmates for years. What about you?

What could you say to the kid you like, without putting pressure on that person?

You may think that sending a note to the kid where you write, "I like you. Write back" is a good idea. But let's think about this. Writing a note means that other kids might see it. Is that what you want? Could that embarrass the other kid (and you), even if that other kid likes you back? Also, the kid who you have a crush on may be too uncomfortable admitting those same feelings back to you, may not be sure how he or she feels, or may not share your feelings.

Evan's Story

Evan liked Sheila, who was in his class. He wrote a script, like a play, to prepare to talk to her. Here is his script:

EVAN: Hey, Sheila. I heard that you like archery.

SHEILA: Yeah. My sister and I take archery lessons. It's not as easy as it looks when the bull's-eye is far away and really small.

EVAN: I've never done it. It looks fun. I'm sure it's hard when you are at your level.

SHEILA: It's not that hard unless you are in competitions. I'm not doing that right now, but I was in a competition last year. I only came in fifth place, though.

EVAN: That's pretty cool that you tried it and fifth place is pretty good.

SHEILA: I guess.

EVAN: If you ever want to teach someone, I'm game. I think it might be fun to try.

SHEILA: Are you serious?

EVAN: Sure, why not? We can go or we can go with a bunch of kids.

SHEILA: Okay. Let me talk with my mom and see if we can do that. Maybe we can have a bunch of kids all go and learn at the same time.

Writing a script doesn't mean the other person will follow it, but it was a way for Evan to prepare for talking with Sheila, and being prepared made him feel more confident as he actually began to have a conversation with her. Evan's script gave Sheila a way to show that she wanted to hang out with him, but that she didn't have to decide to just be with him.

What do you think about the way Evan's script was written? How would you handle a crush? What would your script look like?

So what can you do or say? Here is what Gloria said,

"I had a crush on Harold, a kid in my class. I didn't tell him, but I started hanging around him more. I knew he liked baseball, so I learned more about it and asked his opinion about the different teams. It was fun just talking with him. A few weeks later, when we were hanging and no one was around, I said, "You're fun to talk to." He got all red but said, "Yeah, you too." That's enough for me for now."

Be friends first. It's hard to be patient, though. Today or tomorrow, you can start building on your friendship and seeing how it goes. Remember how to meet a new friend. What would you say to a friend? Try saying it to this person.

Now, if there's a big dance coming up or Valentine's Day or a party that you're both invited to, you might want to casually expand your comfort zone. What could you say to the kid you like, without putting pressure on that person? Here is what Pete said,

"Just for fun, want to be my Valentine?"

And, Joanie said, "On Sadie Hawkins day, the girls are supposed to ask the guys to the school dance. I'm thinking of asking you. Would you go? No pressure."

In both examples, the kids didn't pressure the other person. In fact, if the other kid said no, Peter or Joanie could just shrug their shoulders, smile, and say, "No problem." They can walk away still feeling good about themselves and more confident because they took a risk.

Self-Talk

You know that self-talk means that you have a conversation with yourself. Think of it as your own personal pep talk. The more confidence you feel, the easier it is to take a new risk and handle those new feelings that you may now have for someone else.

So, here's a review of self-talk strategies:

* Be careful not to use words to beat yourself up. ("I'm so stupid. No one will ever like me.")
* Give yourself a pep talk. ("I'm an awesome person already. And I like having a crush. I'll be disappointed if the other kid doesn't like me back, but I'll be okay.")
* Have a positive mental attitude. ("This crush thing is fun. I guess I'm kind of growing up, liking people and all.")
* Use calming strategies, like taking deep breaths and reminding yourself to relax.
* Talk with your friends and support team if you are unsure how to act and for an extra confidence boost.

What will you say to yourself to keep your self-confidence high and to begin to slowly expand your comfort zone and talk with that person who you have a crush on?

What to Expect

If you've ever seen movies where one person confesses love for the other and then music plays in the background and they slowly smile, hold hands, and are amazingly and instantly happy, it's important to remember that this was a movie. In real life, things rarely move that quickly.

If you have a crush on another kid, maybe you also know something about that person. Is that person interested in boys or girls yet? Has this person entered the crush stage? Is that kid nice? Is that kid super popular and only hangs out with other super popular kids? All of this information may give you some idea of the response you might get if you confess your feelings.

Is that person interested in boys or girls yet? Has this person entered the crush stage?

Confessing your feelings doesn't mean that you say that you have a crush on that kid. After all, that could make that kid feel uncomfortable, even if the crush is shared. There are three main responses you can get. You can:

* Get rejected or laughed at
* Get ignored
* Get the answer that the other kid likes you back

What if You've Been Turned Down?

Finding out your crush doesn't feel the same about you can be tough. Here's what Michelle did when she was rejected or ignored:

* I talked to my friends. They helped me feel a lot better.
* I did the stuff I always liked to do, like skateboarding and reading comic books. I just focused on that.
* I told myself that I can still feel good about me, even though he didn't like me like that.

What can you do if things don't turn out like you'd want with your crush?

Would you really want to hang out with a kid who makes you feel bad?

What do you do if you both have a crush? What are the rules?

You might get rejected. If someone rejects you, it may be because that kid isn't ready for a crush, or doesn't want to have that changed relationship with you, or has a crush on someone else. It does NOT mean that you are no longer a valuable person. If the kid laughs at you, then that's actually good information for you. Would you really want to hang out with a kid who makes you feel bad? Time to rethink that crush if this happens.

You might get ignored. If the kid ignores you, it's time to give your crush some space. The kid may be just too uncomfortable with the situation, may give you a response weeks later, or may just want to get to know you as a friend right now.

You might have a mutual crush. If the kid tells you that the crush is mutual (shared), yippee! But now what? This presents its own set of questions. What do you do if you both have a crush? What are the rules? What's expected? Because this may be a new situation for you both, it's a great plan to speak with older people, like your parents or other trusted adults, about what is expected if you both have a crush on each other.

Confidence Boosters

* I'm changing, so it's normal to feel a little nervous.
* If I have a crush, I can just get to be better friends with that kid right now.
* I have a support team to help me through this new experience of liking someone.
* I can still feel confidence in myself, whether or not the other kid likes me back.

Many kids feel a little nervous and a lot excited when they have a crush. It's okay (and natural) to feel a little discomfort. You're expanding your comfort zone. It's helpful to take your time before doing anything with your feelings. You can practice what you might say to that other person, you can ask for help, you can practice self-talk, and you can remain self-confident even if your crush isn't mutual. Now that you know what you might expect when you have a crush, you can be better prepared to take on these new feelings. And have fun with them! In the next chapter, you'll read about how to remain confident when you are in a large group. This is another issue related to social confidence.

Chapter 13

Hang Out With a Group

Maybe you feel confident when you hang out with one or two kids, but what happens when you are with a group?

Some kids feel that it's easy to be in a group. For other kids, being with a group outside of school can mean trying to expand their comfort zones.

In this chapter, you'll read about:

* When to talk and when to listen
* Peer pressure
* Group survival skills

Even if you are used to being in groups, you may pick up a few tips from reading the next few pages.

When to Talk and When to Listen

If you are having lunch with a friend, it's usually easy to figure out when to talk and when to listen. The rules aren't that clear when you are in a group. In groups, you may be with a few kids for hours and rarely speak. You may be listening to music together and no one talks much. Or you may be at a dance and focused on dancing, not talking. But what if kids are talking to each other but not talking directly to you? If you use negative self-talk, you can convince yourself that they don't care about you. Often, that's not the case, though. Kids usually talk with groups of kids, not individuals, when they're together. So, here are a few pointers:

* Don't assume you are being ignored.
* Feel free to chime in with your thoughts when the other kid pauses. It shows that you were listening and want to be an active member of the group.
* Don't feel pressured to talk more than you want to. Many quiet kids are very popular.

If you feel confident that you are okay with you, then other kids may end up being fine with you listening but not talking much. You can participate in many ways, sometimes by showing that you are listening by using your body language, sometimes by just being with the group.

> What if kids are talking to each other but not talking directly to you?

Peer Pressure

Peer pressure is when you feel pressured by other kids to act, think, or feel in certain ways. Robert said, "Kids at school kept bugging me to try out for the football team, just 'cause I liked to fool around and play football at recess. It really bothered me." Now, there is positive

Can you think
of a time when
other kids put
pressure on
you to do
something?

(or good) peer pressure and negative (or bad) peer pressure. Which do you think Robert experienced?

The kids who were pressuring Robert may have either been trying to encourage him (good or positive peer pressure) or set him up for a problem (bad or negative peer pressure). If Robert liked to play football at recess but was always tackled and rarely caught the ball, you may think that kids were suggesting he try out for the team as a sarcastic joke. Not funny! But if Robert was amazing at defense and offense when playing football at recess, you might think that the other kids were just trying to encourage Robert to try out for the team. Does this make sense? As you can see, peer pressure isn't always good or always bad—it can be either. Here's how to differentiate between the two.

Positive Peer Pressure

Not all peer pressure is bad. If some of your friends are pressuring you to sign up for a marine biology after-school activity with them, because they know that you'll like it, then that is good peer pressure. Your friends are trying to encourage you to do something that they think you will enjoy and they want to do it with you. Hopefully, they'll give you little nudges to do it and not really end up bugging you about it.

Friends often encourage each other. But what can you say if you feel that they are pressuring you too much, even though they are doing it to help you?

Here are a few tips for handling positive peer pressure:

* If you want to talk with your friends about putting too much positive peer pressure on you, try role playing what you will say.

Ways to Respond to Peer Pressure

Are you trying to deal with peer pressure? Here are some things that Herbie says to kids who are trying to pressure him:

* I'm not into that.
* I think I'll pass.
* That doesn't sound so good to me. Besides, we could get into a lot of trouble. Let's do something else.
* Maybe another time.
* I can think for myself and I'm not going to do that.

Can you come up with your own things to say? You can practice them and have them ready to use if you're ever feeling pressured.

* Think about what your friends are saying, then decide if it's right for you. When you're hanging with a group, sometimes a lot of kids try to encourage you to do something positive.
* Be clear in what you're going to do and let them know you appreciate their advice.
* Try not to sound like you are accusing them of bugging you. That never goes over well!

What can you say if you feel your friends are pressuring you too much, even though they are doing it to help you?

Negative Peer Pressure

Negative peer pressure is usually when kids, maybe even some of your friends, try to get you to do something that you know is not good for you. Sometimes this happens more when you are hanging with a group because the other kids get carried away with the power of the group and the need to be accepted. If everyone does something negative, then they can convince themselves that it was okay. Does this make sense?

Maybe they want you to take unhealthy risks, like smoking or cutting classes. If a kid you hardly know tries to convince you to smoke, it might be easy for you to decide to say no. But what if it's a group of friends?

Here are a few strategies for dealing with peer pressure:

* Decide if it's positive or negative, then decide to avoid the negative.
* Remind yourself that true friends won't keep pressuring you to do something negative if you let them know how you feel.
* Tell yourself that you are cool as you are and don't have to give in to pressure.
* Stay calm (use the calming strategies).
* Practice lines to say if you face negative peer pressure.

Standing Up to Peer Pressure

Sometimes you can try to avoid peer pressure, and try to be respectful of the other kids, but still end up with a conflict. Life sometimes involves problems and conflicts. If you stand up for yourself, you may find that some people don't always agree with you. Going along with the crowd, even when you won't feel good about yourself for doing this, is easy at first. But kids usually end up feeling uncomfortable and disappointed in themselves if they keep making choices that they aren't happy about. Here's what Henry said,

If everyone does something negative, then they can convince themselves that it was okay. Does this make sense?

"One of my best friends told me to drink beer at his party or I'm not cool. I thought about it, but it didn't feel right. I told him that I'm already cool, so he should just chill. He smiled and said, 'Your loss!' but was fine with me the rest of the night."

Standing up to peer pressure may mean losing a friend. But was that kid a true friend if he or she wouldn't accept your refusal to give in to peer pressure? Feeling self-confident means that you feel good about yourself and your choices. Don't let anyone take that away from you by pressuring you!

Was that kid a true friend if he or she wouldn't accept your refusal to give in to peer pressure?

Group Survival Skills

When you hang out in a group, there are some skills that you will find helpful. Here are a few of those skills:

* Don't interrupt people while they're still talking.
* Use positive body language and look directly at the person.
* Become comfortable being quiet.
* Try not to insult other kids or lecture them when you're resisting negative peer pressure.
* Try inviting everyone to your home sometimes (if it's okay with your parents), especially if you often get invited to the homes of other kids.

Along with these skills, here are a few things to remember and tell yourself:

* The group should make you feel good and comfortable. If it's the right group for you, you shouldn't have to change your personality to fit in.
* Be true to yourself. Don't go along with the group just because everyone else is doing something.

Kaylie's Story

Kaylie had been at the mall with a bunch of her friends who shoplifted from a store. Kaylie didn't shoplift and was upset that her friends did. She asked her dad what she should do. Kaylie hoped that her dad would give her the quick answer and not ask any questions. But he asked lots of questions. He said, "It's not easy to come up with one answer. You don't want to lecture other kids, but if you let them know that you are worried or concerned, you still may risk getting your friends mad. Sometimes, you just have to take that risk, though."

Her father had suggested that she talk to each friend alone, so they wouldn't be self-conscious. The next day, Kaylie spoke with two of her friends. But before she did, Kaylie reminded herself that she was confident and was going to feel good that she was doing the right thing, even if her friends didn't agree.

Then she talked to her friends. "I've been thinking a lot about yesterday. I think almost everyone ended up taking the dare and taking something from that store." Kaylie didn't remind her friends that she didn't take anything—she didn't want to make them feel even worse. She told her friends, "I think it's hard to say no to things sometimes, when we're all together in such a big group and Andrea comes up with her brilliant ideas. She makes them sound exciting. But I don't want us to get in trouble. Can we make a pact that we'll stick together and not do that stuff?"

Kaylie held her breath after talking with both of her friends. She knew that each of them might feel mad at or hurt by her. But she wanted to put some positive peer pressure on them and she knew that a pact was a good idea because there's power in numbers. Kaylie's friends admitted that they were embarrassed about what they did at the mall and thought the pact was a great idea.

How would you have handled Kaylie's dilemma?

* If a friend is doing something dangerous in a group, talk to her and try to help her make a healthier decision (although your friend eventually has to make her own decision).

Remember to make sure you're surrounded by people you're comfortable with. Then it's easier to find your own style for mingling with the group.

There are a bunch of differences between talking with one friend and talking when you're with a group of kids. It's a whole new dynamic. Along with groups can come positive peer pressure and possibly negative peer pressure. We talked about some techniques for handling each. You also learned some quick tips for being in a group.

Confidence Boosters

* I like me, so I don't need to act differently just to fit in.
* Positive peer pressure may make me uncomfortable, but I should think about it before I say no.
* Going places and doing new things with friends can make the new experience even more fun and feel safer.

Keep on Growing

As you go through the next few months, and years, go back over the chapters and practice the ways that you can build up your confidence.

Here are a few reminders:

* Make a list of your strengths.
* You don't need to be the best, but it is important to try your best.
* Remember that you are special because you are you!
* Try to learn from your mistakes—even confident people can make them!
* Acting as if you're confident can help you feel confident.
* Compliment yourself each time you have the confidence to take a small step outside of your comfort zone.

* Rely on your support team—you are not alone!
* Speak up for yourself, share your opinion, and find others who appreciate you.
    * Be ready for bumps in the road.
        * Remember that therapists are experts on helping kids and can help you work on improving your confidence level and self-esteem.

Reading this book is a big step forward. I hope you've gained the knowledge and tools to start building up your confidence.

Congratulations and good luck.

About the Author

Wendy L. Moss, PhD, ABPP, FAASP, has her doctorate in clinical psychology, is a licensed psychologist, and has a certification in school psychology. Dr. Moss has practiced in the field of psychology for over 25 years and has worked in hospital, residential, private practice, clinic, and school settings. She has the distinction of being recognized as a diplomate in school psychology by the American Board of Professional Psychology for her advanced level of competence in the field of school psychology. Dr. Moss has been appointed as a fellow in the American Academy of School Psychology.

In addition, she is the author of *Children Don't Come With an Instruction Manual: A Teacher's Guide to Problems That Affect Learners* and has written several articles. Dr. Moss is currently an ad hoc reviewer for the *Journal for Specialists in Group Work* and the *Journal of School Psychology*.

About Magination Press

Magination Press publishes self-help books for kids and the adults in their lives. We are an imprint of the American Psychological Association, the largest scientific and professional organization representing psychologists in the United States and the largest association of psychologists worldwide.